M000041831

ROAD
TO THE
TOP

ROAD TO THE TOP

The Chief Executive Officer in Canada

by

Alexander R. Aird, Paul Nowack
and James W. Westcott

Doubleday Canada Limited, Toronto

Canadian Cataloguing in Publication Data

Nowack, Paul
   Road to the top: the chief executive officer in Canada
ISBN 0-385-25140-8

1. Organizational effectiveness.   2. Success in business.
3. Chief executive officers – Canada.
I. Westcott, James.   II. Aird, Alexander.
III. Title.

HD38.25.C3N68 1988   655.4'09   C88-093098-5

DESIGN AND PAGEMAKEUP: Brant Cowie/Artplus Limited

COVER DESIGN: David Wyman Design

TYPE OUTPUT: Tony Gordon Ltd.

Printed and bound in Canada
by T. H. Best Printing Company Limited

Published in Canada by
Doubleday Canada Limited
105 Bond Street
Toronto, Ontario
M5B 1Y3

C O N T E N T S

PREFACE

"Chief Executives" — the very words exude an aura of strength, power, wealth. They are the leaders of our business society, but they are for the most part invisible, faceless, and unknown — shadowy figures whom most Canadians never meet, let alone know as friends or acquaintances.

This is a gap of some significance, for the top professional managers — the "hired guns" of Canadian business — control decisions that can alter the lives of thousands of employees, threaten the existence of whole towns, and affect the long-term health of our economy. They deserve to be better known.

For too long CEOs have been neglected by our business writers and journalists. Our business schools, from which most of today's CEOs have graduated, teach little about the job of the chief executive. Most of them have been left to find the "Road to the Top" on their own.

This volume, written by two widely experienced and respected business consultants and a business journalist, attempts to redress the situation. Based on the authors' extensive personal contacts, it brings these CEOs to life, revealing them as intensely human, intelligent and thoughtful individuals, reflective about their jobs and careers, and occasionally regretful at the sacrifices that have been made in getting there. On the surface, they appear recognizable and ordinary — the guy next door — sharing the same origins, doubts and failures as many of the rest of us. But at the same time there is a thread of single-mindedness and toughness that runs like a *leitmotiv* throughout their often frank and revealing statements about their lives and careers. In this regard, they are any-thing but ordinary.

Road to the Top is a welcome addition to Canadian busi-ness literature. It provides valuable insights into the reality of the job, and the personalities and outlooks of the Canadians who have made it. It portrays a demanding life, and an often lonely one, accurately, sensitively and with great understanding.

David S. R. Leighton
National Centre for Management
Research and Development
London, Ontario

ACKNOWLEDGEMENTS

The authors are indebted to many people for their contributions to the preparation of this book. First and foremost are those fifty CEOs who permitted us to interview them specifically for the book. Without their willingness to discuss their careers and ideas openly and honestly this project would have been impossible. We wish also to thank the many unnamed executives and managers who over nearly thirty years of our professional experience have discussed their careers and aspirations with us. Our contacts with these people formed the basis of many of the observations and ideas which are in the book. Additional thanks are due to a group of rising women executives who met with us to discuss their experiences and attitudes related to their particular roads to the top.

The production of the book turned out to be much more onerous than any of us had anticipated, and were it not for the help and encouragement of a number of people we might not have achieved it at all. Our editor, Jennifer Glossop, displayed a wonderful amalgam of tact, patience and toughness. Dennis Adair and Janet Rosenstock were very helpful in the arrangement of the diverse material which has gone into this book. Nancy Westcott contributed greatly by her transcriptions of interviews, careful reading of the many versions of the manuscript, encouragement and tough criticisms. Lin Cullen, Sandy Aird's assistant, in addition to her usual tasks, transcribed a number of interviews and kept track of masses of material. Dr. Donald Franklin gave valuable help with the statistical analyses of enormous quantities of data and their interpretation.

We wish also to thank our families and business associates who encouraged us and made it possible to find the time required for the book.

Any book that offers comment, analysis and judgement on management and, indeed, on the individuals who reach the top job will inevitably provoke critical comment about omissions and errors of judgement. We accept this and in fact welcome it. Our objective from the outset has been to explain and reveal the dimensions of the job and the people who have made it to the top. If our book generates interest and discussion, then we shall have achieved our purpose.

ROAD TO THE TOP

INTRODUCTION

THE
TOP JOB

This book is about a job and the people who do it. The job itself is called many things, but perhaps the best description is the "top job." The title assigned to those who hold the top job at major companies varies and has changed over time, but in most corporate structures of the 1980s, the person (although he may also carry the title "chairman," "president" or "vice president") is called "chief executive officer" (CEO), a title that usually designates the person who is responsible for running the business and is accountable to a board of directors and shareholders.

Canada's major capitalists—the Bronfmans, the Reichmans, the Irvings—still control huge organizations, but size, rapidly changing technology and the need for specialization have made it exceedingly difficult for them to make management decisions. In most cases, these matters are left to professional managers; the companies may belong to the owners, but it is the executives, the specialists and the experts who operate them. And the leaders of these management teams are, in most Canadian corporations, the chief executive officers.

The range of a CEO's responsibility is awesome. Put simply, the person at the top is accountable to the board, to the company's shareholders and, indirectly, to the public. The CEO is also held responsible for every aspect of the company's performance, from its safety record to its market share and its return on investment. No matter what the size of the company, the CEO's responsibility is the same. The CEO who presides over a multinational with twenty subsidiary companies, two hundred plants across the world and a labor force that exceeds the population of a small city (Bell Canada Enterprises, Canada's largest corporate employer, has 110,000 employees) shares the same accountability to his board of directors as the chief executive officer of a publicly held company with one plant and 200 employees. Whatever the industry or size of the operation, the buck stops at the CEO's desk.

In addition, all CEOs are judged by the same measures of corporate performance: quality of products or services, innovativeness, competitiveness, current financial status, use of corporate assets, long-term investment value, labor relations, capacity to attract and develop talented employees, quality of management and community and environment responsibility.

In our careers in management consulting and the media, we have met and worked with a large number of CEOs in Canada and the United States. In some cases, our relationships were purely professional and related only to particular assignments, which have ranged from personnel management advice and career counseling through complex corporate strategic planning and organizational restructuring. In other cases, casual friendships developed. As we got to know these people as individuals, they told us about their personal attitudes and about their feelings concerning their jobs, their lives and their families.

We were intrigued on three counts. First, we were surprised to learn how little most people know about the job itself and about the functional and analytical skills required of a chief executive officer. Even less, we realized, was known about the CEOs themselves, their backgrounds, their values, their attitudes and their motivations. Had they planned their careers? How had they managed to rise through the corporate ranks? Second, we wondered what amalgam of intelligence, insight, knowledge and personal skills had allowed them to achieve the top job. What was it that distinguished these people from those who did not reach the top? Are such business leaders born or are the necessary characteristics developed over time? Is there anything special about these men, or have they just been lucky? And third, we became interested in the job itself. What management practices are involved? Can CEOs, who are essentially removed from the factory floor, take the company in new directions? Do CEOs tend to structure their jobs and relate to their boards of directors in similar ways and do they use the same support systems?

This book attempts to answer these and other questions about chief executive officers and the people who occupy the most powerful and the most demanding job in business. Many of the insights and judgements are ours: after nearly thirty years in consulting practice, we have naturally developed our own views about CEOs and their performances. But the material in this book is also the product of interviews with CEOs themselves. In the past three years we have talked to fifty CEOs of major Canadian corporations. (A complete list is found in the Appendix.)

We are interested in those CEOs who manage a company whose ownership is controlled by others, and we have excluded from consideration those who manage companies they started or inherited. Our interest is in the professional manager who has worked his way to the top job. To the best of our knowledge, there is currently no woman in Canada who manages a large or even moderate-sized company for someone else. Angela Cantwell Peters, who until her retirement (upon the sale of the company) was chairman and CEO of Bowering Brothers Limited, is the only woman we have been able to identify in this role. (This is the reason for our use of the male pronoun in referring to CEOs.) Yet it is clear from the appointment notices in the newspapers that women are reaching increasingly higher executive levels, even if not yet the top job of CEO. There are some very prominent and successful women

CEOs in Canada; they all, however, enjoy a strong or controlling equity position.

It is not surprising that women have not yet reached the position of CEO as we define it. Most men are made CEOs of their companies in their fifties, and twenty-five or thirty years ago there were few women entering business in the occupations or functions that most often lead to the top job. In our opinion, this has already changed radically, and we feel that there will soon be female CEOs as the current generation of business executives reaches the top job age group. This view is supported by our interviews with many CEOs and with a number of women in the executive ranks. It is because of this that we have written a chapter to highlight the characteristics, issues and experience relating to upwardly mobile women.

In spite of our many combined years of working with CEOs, some of the things we discovered in the course of preparing this book did surprise us. For example, we found it hard to believe the fact that so many of the CEOs had not really planned to get the top job, but simply took one step at a time.

It is our hope that the reader will find some new ideas, some insights into the top job and into the characteristics, careers and attitudes of the CEOs, and that these insights will help the reader to develop his—and, increasingly, her—career.

P A R T

1

MYTHS AND
REALITIES

*The popular image of the leader of a major
corporation is often more myth than
reality. We devote the first section of this
book to putting the facts straight, to
examining the years of preparation
necessary to travel the road to the top, and
to describing how, once there, the
successful CEO grasps his new
responsibilities.*

1

THE MYTH
AND THE
REALITY

W hat image does the title "chief executive officer" con-
jure up in the public mind? How does the average
person regard these powerful, high-salaried men? Are they
and their values admired by the public? Finally, do many
CEOs have a public image?

The public tends to build stereotyped profiles of people
in business and the professions. Bankers are often
described as gray men in pin-striped suits; lawyers are
conservative professionals in blue suits; while stockbrokers
are photographed on the job, a trifle frenzied, with rolled-
up shirt sleeves and loosened ties.

But what about the chief executive officer of a major
corporation? No specific appearance springs to mind, no
ready stereotypic image is suggested. This is because the
chief executive officers of Canadian corporations are largely unknown men who, unlike politicians and other in-
fluential members of our society, often avoid public exposure.

Yet consider their impact as heads of Canadian corporations. In 1986 there were twenty-five Canadian corporations (none government-owned) with annual operating revenues of more than $3 billion. Together they accounted for revenues that total approximately $170 billion while controlling assets in excess of $135 billion. More than 700,000 people work for those twenty-five corporate groups. To these figures you can add a further $450 billion plus in assets and another 170,000 employees by simply including Canada's five largest banking corporations and five biggest life-insurance companies. If one adds all the employees included in the *Financial Post 500* survey of Canada's five hundred largest industrials and one hundred largest financial institutions, the number of employees well exceeds two million.

The impact of Canada's top corporations is, to say the least, significant. Obviously, the men who head them have a great deal of influence over our everyday lives, yet if asked to name a single Canadian CEO, the average Canadian might have difficulty. So, to a large extent, would the average American, although Americans might name Chrysler Corporation's Lee Iacocca.

The chief executive officer of Chrysler is in many ways typical of other CEOs, but he is unique in one important aspect: Lee Iacocca has a public persona. He is seen doing his own commercials for Chrysler; he is the author of a best-selling autobiography and he is frequently mentioned in various publications. He is so well known that we are aware, for example, that in one recent year he earned $11 million in salary, bonus and stock from Chrysler. Given this astronomical income, it is hardly surprising that people flocked to buy his book. How does a man attain this kind of financial success while working for someone else? The public also knows a great deal about Lee Iacocca's personal life—that is, his life outside the Chrysler Corporation. The press filled us in on the details of his marriage and, eight months later, his divorce. We were told about his political ambitions and we witnessed his role in the Statue of Liberty fund-raising committee.

But Iacocca is a rare exception. Most CEOs do not become public figures. They are not prepared for publicity, or for the criticism that comes with sharing their success with the public.

More often than not, when a CEO becomes publicly visible, it is because he has stumbled into fame—or notoriety—or has taken a strong public position on some matter. One such Canadian CEO is Adam Zimmerman, chairman of MacMillan Bloedel Ltd. and president of Noranda Inc., which controls MacMillan Bloedel. In 1986, at the time of the lumber tariff controversy, Mr. Zimmerman emerged as a spokesperson for the lumber industry and appeared on television and radio and in the press. He was described by the Toronto *Star* as "a man of great frankness, clarity and talent for the memorable phrase." The same article continued, "Almost overnight winning one of the highest profiles, among Canadian businessmen, Zimmerman provided the nucleus for drama."

Yet, despite Zimmerman's high profile, the public knew very little about him outside his corporate position and his stand on a specific issue. Most CEOs are not motivated by a desire for public recognition. Rather, they are more concerned about earning the respect of their peers and those who work for and with them.

The way CEOs view their public-relations role depends on how they got the top job. There are two common routes to the top: some work their way up in one company and stay on as CEO, presumably until they retire; others move from one company to another as they ascend to the top job and even then continue to move on as new opportunities come their way.

Donald McIvor, formerly CEO of Imperial Oil Limited and now senior vice-president and director of Exxon Corporation, is a company man who rose through the ranks of the corporation. Like others who have stayed in one company, McIvor was initially not particularly aware of the public-relations aspect of his role as chief executive officer. He fully understood the importance of his image within the company, but not outside the company, in the political forum, for example. But these days oil is politics, and the

CEO of any oil company can expect to be in the public eye. Moreover, in his new position as the head of one of the largest companies in Canada, McIvor was invited to join boards of directors of other companies and industry associations. He also faced a major new challenge dealing with the media.

McIvor approached his need for an image in a planned and disciplined way. When he became chief executive officer of Imperial Oil, he met with public-relations executives of the company to discuss what sort of public image he should have and how he should go about developing it. Don McIvor is by nature a quiet, rather retiring and unassuming person. His advisors chose an effective yet somewhat daring approach. They arranged a series of informal but on-the-record lunches with leading business journalists, at which McIvor candidly explained his position on various issues. This approach suited McIvor and resulted in mutual respect between McIvor and the business media. He said, "When the media phone, I take the call."

The other type of CEO—the man hired into the company—will stay in a company as long as he sees it taking him to his ultimate goal. If he is blocked, he will move when he is offered a better opportunity. These men are usually much more aware of the importance of image than a man like Donald McIvor. They see themselves as a product and they have a good sense of how to merchandize themselves.

F. Ross Johnson, now chief executive officer of RJR Nabisco Inc., is such a man. He says, "What's the use of being in an organization if you aren't going to run it?" And from early on in his life, he has aimed for the top and cultivated his image. At the University of Manitoba, he joined a fraternity where he did all the jobs from assistant rushing chairman to president of his fraternity and his class, and he did them well—but he kept his eye on the top job, and what he had to do to get it.

As a young accountant with Canadian General Electric, he joined one of the most exclusive golf clubs in Toronto even though he could not really afford it at the time. He knew, however, that the club would help him meet people and make contacts with senior executives whom he would not meet in the course of his job. To be seen by the right people is important. For Johnson, a natural athlete, golf was an ideal choice. From the very beginning he cultivated the image of the man on the way up.

To both types of CEO, the most important image is the one they have among their peers—not the public. And the criteria on which they want to be judged are their effectiveness and their business acumen, be these measured by market share, net profit, return on equity or the strength of the balance sheet.

Since so little accurate information is presented to the public, certain myths have developed about CEOs. Many people assume that CEOs reached for the top in order to attain wealth. We have not found this to be true. Money was not the overwhelming motivation for most CEOs, although it was a consideration. To Melvin Hawkrigg, president and CEO of Trilon Financial Corporation, who spent fourteen years working his way up from an accounting job to president of the Fuller Brush Company before moving to the financial-services business, money has been one of three important components in his career:

> I am motivated by money. I don't apologize for it because I want the good things for my family. I want the good things in life and I want to have my share of them if I can. But I rank achievement on the job and personal development ahead of money.

When asked how important money is to him, Peter Gordon, former CEO of Stelco Inc., replied:

> Absolutely not important. Never in my life have I asked for an increase. Certainly there have been occasions when I wished I had more money, but I always felt the people I worked for would recognize what I was doing and my contribution with compensation. I still maintain that feeling. I hate to have somebody come to me and say, "Pete, you should be paying me X dollars more than you are." I feel that's a failing on my part, or on his superior's part. We

should be able to recognize what someone is worth, and when I hear that so-and-so asked for an increase, it worries me a bit that the organization has missed this, or that he perceives himself as worth more. But money has never been that important to me.

Although CEOs agree that money is not the prime motivation, they disagree when asked what is most important. Louis Hollander, CEO of Canada Colors and Chemicals, said, "The big motivator for me is the personal opportunity for building an organization which is growing profitable and meets human needs."

Laurent Beaudoin, CEO of Bombardier Inc., described his prime motivation:

What drives me is mainly building an organization that will last. My challenge has been different from some others because in Quebec we have not had a real manufacturing base. My challenge is to build one that will last for those coming after. The company enjoyed a tremendous growth in the seventies. Then I realized that everything we had built could disappear. Should that have happened, for me personally, I could have gone through it without financial problems. What motivated me to stay and overcome the situation was the loyalty of all the people working for the company. The thing that is most important is people.

Maurice Jodoin, CEO of General Trustco, reflected the most generally held attitude of the CEOs we interviewed. He simply loves what he does. He enjoys the accoutrements that go with the job, but he does not want just the money or power. To him working is not work. His goal has simply been to achieve the CEO level of responsiblity.

Even if making money is not their prime motivation, most CEOs do earn large salaries and have additional income from stock and bonuses. The total compensation package of the typical Canadian CEO who runs a medium-sized firm with annual sales of $133 million is $293,000 a year including cash bonuses, perks, benefits and incentives, according to a 1986 worldwide survey conducted by Towers, Perrin, Forster and Crosby.

Compared to their peers in other countries, they are not that well paid. In fact, the typical Canadian CEO ranked seventh in compensation compared to CEOs in ten countries. They were paid 40 percent less than their American counterparts. The American CEO earned $391,000 a year in salary and benefits. According to a survey of 142 senior executives at thirty major Canadian companies by the *Financial Times* of Canada executives enjoyed an average gain of 19 percent in 1986, compared to 6 percent the previous year.

While that may seem remarkable in a year in which the economy grew just 3 percent, and corporate profits fell 12.5 percent, most of the gain did not come from salary increases. The big money came from executives exercising stock options to cash in on the vibrant bull market, and from increased bonuses and awards. The cash compensation for these executives rose 10.4 percent in 1986. That was still well above the average wage gain of 3.4 percent negotiated by organized labor in 1986.

Of the thirty companies surveyed by the *Financial Times*, three CEOs collected more than $1 million in company-related compensation. These individuals—George Albino, chairman, president and CEO of Rio Algom Limited, Edmund Fitzgerald chairman and CEO of Northern Telecom Canada Limited and David Culver, president and CEO, Alcan Aluminum Limited—led their counterparts by a wide margin.

The amount of money CEOs (and senior executives) earn tends to make the general public suspicious. On this point our language betrays us. Money, we are told, is the root of all evil, and we therefore assume that someone who has a lot of money probably earned it in nefarious ways. This brings up another myth: CEOs are not nice and their values differ considerably from those of the public in general. This myth is partially true, since some values the public sees as negative are viewed as essential within the culture of the corporation. On the other hand, some values, such as honesty, are important both inside and outside the corporation.

However, many characteristics seen as virtues in the corporate world are seen as less than virtuous or even immoral by the general public. Values, especially those related to keeping costs low, are most often the target of the public's judgment. If employees must be laid off to make a specific section of the firm cost-efficient in order to avoid a plant closure, then the effective manager will lay them off. But the general public may view this act as "mean" and possibly immoral. This discrepancy poses problems for CEOs.

John Fraser, president and chief executive officer of Federal Industries Ltd. a Winnipeg based conglomerate, believes that senior managers all too often abdicate their leadership role when tough decisions must be made because, as he put it, "Far too many of us get caught up in trying to do what we think society expects us to do, and that all too often leads us to rationalize—or compromise—our way out of difficult challenges instead of confronting them." The result, according to Fraser, is a corporate malaise with consequences that range from declining productivity to a serious erosion of our competitive position in international markets, all caused by a long-term decline in business integrity. Fraser distinguishes between business integrity and ethics. Integrity, he says, is a guiding force within us, a firm acceptance of a code, while ethics refers to accepted standards of conduct.

Most CEOs are guided by ethical considerations. If they are guided only by concern about public acceptance, senior managers may, for example allow inventories to build rather than lay off employees; they may authorize bonuses despite a year of bleak sales; or they may find ways to keep an incompetent manager because of a sense of loyalty. The result? Profits shrink or disappear, creditors call outstanding loans and the only option is to close a plant, thereby devastating the company, its employees and the community.

Fraser stated, "We can't have world class, highly competitive and profitable business enterprises without great business leaders—men and women with inner toughness—the kind of leaders who know what has to be done and have the courage and integrity to do it."

There is a myth that once an executive reaches the top of the corporation and takes the chief executive officer's chair, he has it easy because he is in the driver's seat. Well, it just isn't so. Today, major corporations are large and complex organizations, and today's CEOs must understand and deal with the corporation's employees, its structure and its spirit.

Twenty years ago, the behavior of employees was usually both predictable and controllable; today it is far less so. Human rights legislation, contract agreements negotiated by professional organizations or unions, government pressure, and even the new structure of families have caused dramatic changes in the employee-employer relationship. Yesterday's employee would probably have agreed to move almost anywhere to ensure his or her advancement. Today's employees are quite different. He or she is well aware that moving personal possessions is costly, that housing in Toronto or Vancouver is far more expensive than the same type of housing in Winnipeg. The child-care arrangements may be more difficult in Edmonton than in Montreal. Or the spouse may become unemployed, thus reducing the family income. We are witnessing a very important change in the motivation and attitudes of the people who work in corporations. Once, employees might have been motivated by a love for their job or by the prospect of future security, but today, as recently shown by a Toronto *Star* poll, the vast majority of those questioned about why they work responded, "For the money."

Setting a tone that provides for the effective management, motivation and development of good people in an organization is a very complex task today. Steven Wilgar, chief executive officer of Warner-Lambert Canada Inc., put it succinctly:

> You need people to accomplish things. You can have all the strategy in the world, but unless you've got the right people doing the right jobs nothing can happen.

David Clark, CEO of Campbell Soup Company Limited, reinforced the importance of people in the work of the chief executive officer:

The thing that is most satisfying is working to unleash the human capabilities of your people. It is enormously hard work, and you've got to work at it a million and one ways every minute of the day. Virtually everything you do has to be oriented around it one way or another. If you do that, and if you have good people to start with, it will seed the rest of the organization and give you some successes that you can point to for the rest of the organization. If you do that, by God, it works!

Having the right people is one thing. Having them in the right place doing the right thing at the right time is another. That requires a structure. Every corporation has a structure. That structure is defined and described in many ways: on organization charts, in position descriptions, in policy manuals, in systems and procedures, in rules and regulations, in parking-lot arrangements, in benefits programs and so on. The structure doesn't just happen. It is usually the result of careful, ongoing consideration and analysis, usually managed at the very top of the organization.

In some corporations a functional structure, which distinguishes between the major functions such as production, sales, finance, personnel, research and so on, is the most appropriate. Corporations that are highly sensitive to their markets and offer a variety of products directed toward different customers often prefer the product or business-unit structure, which organizes the human resources of the company in and around particular product lines or businesses. A geographic structure is frequently favored by service corporations where frequent customer contact and close proximity between company and customer are desirable. Usually the structure chosen is the one the chief executive officer is most comfortable with, and which facilitates the way he likes to operate.

Having the right people in the right place isn't the only thing the chief executive officer has to deal with. He is the leader of the organization and it is his job to create and sustain the spirit of enterprise. The spirit or culture of a corporation is, in part, the result of traditions built up over a number of years. It is reflected in the morals and values of the corporation. Spirit is also the product of the industry in which the corporation is engaged. Thus, the spirit of enterprise that one finds at Stelco or Chrysler is different from that found at Avon Cosmetics. We have found that a key ingredient to the development of a spirit of enterprise is often the management style of the chief executive officer. The way this individual conducts himself in the organization and the values he stands for often set the tone for the entire operation.

Irving Ludmer, CEO of Steinberg Inc., a major Quebec-based grocery retailer and conglomerate, said:

> I think it is the CEO who shapes the company. I think people follow the CEO's example. If somebody comes in and works like hell, then others around that person feel they can't let this one person do everything. They perceive it as not being fair, and they start working harder. If the culture is one of integrity, one of cooperativeness with the labor unions, you hear the language start to change. I can talk to you all I like about corporate culture, but it doesn't change overnight, there is a great deal of resistance and skepticism and testing that goes on. The process takes years.

Ludmer went on to describe how the culture of the grocery operation had to change a few years ago:

> It was obvious that we had to get the fellow with the white apron back again, instead of the fancy suit. It wasn't the store manager's fault, it was the fault of the company in the way we had so rigidly bureaucratized the whole thing. We had to give them freedom to do things again and to let them make mistakes. That meant they had to work with their team, with their people. They had to be convinced that cashiers and clerks had brains and knew what the customers wanted because they were talking to them all day. We needed an entrepreneurial store team to combat the independents. The independent is a businessman who has his team. He involves them because he knows that's the only way for him to make a buck. If we could get our

people to act the same way, we would have reduced our strategic disadvantage of being bureaucratic while competing against entrepreneurs.

Robert Morison, CEO of Consumers Packaging Inc., talked about setting the working environment:

> I often get mad when I see evaluations and performance reports on my people and read the words, "The problem with this guy is that he can't motivate anybody." I submit to you that I can't motivate you to do anything. All I can do is put you in an environment in which you yourself will be motivated, and there's a hell of a big difference. A CEO can choose the environment in which the corporation exists. I try to do that in our company in my own way. I think the CEO has a large responsibility to set the tone. A guy's in trouble out there, in marketing or somewhere, and you go out in the morning and go get a cup of coffee or something and you say, "Hey! Hi, John, how are you? How's it going?" "I'm pressed. I've got this problem." I say, "Hey, just stay with it. You'll beat it. You'll be OK. Let's go on." The environmental setting of the corporation to me is very important, because all I can do is influence the long term.

People, structure and spirit are all elements of the complex organization of a corporation, and it is no easy task to stay on top of them all in a positive way. In addition, today's chief executive officers must deal with a whole new set of factors in the external environment, all of which have a direct impact on the survival and growth of their corporations. Twenty years ago the chief executive officer had to respond to only a limited number of groups outside the corporation: shareholders, unions, suppliers and customers. For the most part these groups were predictable and, more significantly, somewhat controllable. Shareholders expected good profits, unions wanted reasonable negotiations, suppliers expected payment and customers wanted satisfaction and quality service.

Today there are other factors, which are not so easily controlled or satisfied. First, there is the government. Rarely can an organization make a decision today that does not in some way require compliance with regulations of one of the three levels of government. Second, there are consumer groups and environmental pressure groups, which have become increasingly vocal in the past ten years. Then there are such other external factors as energy policies, interest rates and government spending; and beyond our borders there are the international pressures, including concentration of assets in a few hands, nationalization, foreign-exchange fluctuations, even the possible destruction of assets through revolution and war.

Closer to home, unions, which traditionally accepted the idea that they should bargain for all they could get and allow management to run the business, however badly, are changing their attitudes. They are beginning to challenge management on a wider range of issues. At the other end of the spectrum are the shareholders, particularly large institutional investors, who are today alleging that some managers hide behind the cloak of social responsibility to entrench themselves in their jobs and deflect criticism of their poor performance.

The chief executive officer, the man at the top, is expected to provide stable management with consistency and foresight. That is not easy. It involves giving leadership and direction to an organization comprised of people within a structure operating within a certain spirit of enterprise and trying to do so in an increasingly complex and difficult market environment.

Another myth, one that has some truth to it, states that those who make it to the top came from the right families, went to the right schools and knew the right people.

The truth is that while the origins of the chief executives are gradually changing to reflect the diversity of the country economically, ethnically and geographically, some 75 percent of the fathers of CEOs were white-collar workers, that is, from the middle class, and nine out of ten started their own careers in white-collar jobs. Thus, while the current selection of CEOs is more varied than one would have found in the last generation, that "good start" still helps.

On the other hand, the matter of schooling has greatly changed. There is an increased tendency for CEOs to come out of public rather than private schools, although work at the graduate level is often completed in a private American university. And law and engineering degrees, which used to be the preferred degrees for a CEO, have given way to the master of business administration degree.

In general then, today's CEOs come from neither great wealth (unless they are inheritors) nor great poverty. They have not been the beneficiaries of an elite education. They come from the middle class.

Most people assume that when people reach the top of the corporate ladder, they have control over their time. This leads to the popular assumption that they spend a lot of time playing golf or tennis, or lying on a sandy palm-lined beach. This brings us to the last myth: the chief executive officer is a man of leisure.

Thomas Galt, chairman and CEO of Sun Life Assurance Company of Canada, describes his alleged life of leisure:

> **Interviewer:** "Has the job had much impact on your private life?"
> **Galt:** "Yes, it has eliminated it. I used to do a lot of skeet shooting. I have done it twice a year since I became president, instead of once a week. Sure, I have always taken holidays, but when I am in town on Saturdays or Sundays, I go to the office. I often work at home. It is a seven-day-a-week job."
> **Interviewer:** "So there isn't any personal life?"
> **Galt:** "Basically there is no clear division between the personal and working parts of my life. Most of the social functions I go to are part or all business. I have trouble finding time to read a book except on an airplane."

Not that these men are complaining. They love their work and enjoy the long hours and constant challenge.

When we began this study of Canadian chief executive officers, we ourselves had a few preconceptions about the people who hold the job. We expected to discover that a high value was placed on material achievement. It is not. We expected to find that the men at the top are deep thinkers. On the whole they are not; they are instead primarily men of action. We thought many would be introspective, and again they are not. They have little or no time for introspection and self-analysis. We thought they might talk about how their siblings or family rivalry spurred them on. This, too, was absent. We also thought many might be religious. There was, in fact, little mention of religion.

Our experience has taught us that the well-worn stereotypes of powerful business leaders are fictions. Yet they continue to be perpetuated in popular media as comfortable clichés. The reality is that the men we interviewed represented a group whose values, aspirations, personalities and motivations are not only different from the popular image, but often are a direct contradiction of it. More surprising is the fact that although these men differ in age, family background, education and skills, their careers often followed similar pattens of development. There are indeed roads to the top. However, the reality is that how well and how easily one travels on them is as much a question of dedication as it is of preparation.

CHAPTER

2

EARLY
YEARS

Has the road to the top been prepared in some special way for most of the individuals who ascend to the chief executive officer's job? Are people who reach the top born with silver spoons in their mouths? Are they different in any significant way from those whose careers plateau and who are regarded as not having the "right stuff"?

Certainly some CEOs come from homes that most would consider to be privileged, but others come from a wide range of economic origins.

André Charron, formerly CEO of Lévesque, Beaubien recalled his need to earn money at an early age:

My father was very liberal, not checking on what I was doing, except reading my school reports and making a few comments. I was quite free and on my own at all times. But, since he was not a wealthy person he could not provide me with pocket money so I started working at an early stage doing all kinds of things to raise a few pennies. I remember, I even sold cats to neighbors when I was ten years of age. I used to sell empty bottles. I would pick up

all the empty bottles I could find and raise a few pennies. I
had to work, I mean I *had* to work. I would find jobs all the
time, I would never stay doing nothing. I started working
on road work in the summers when I was sixteen.

With many of the CEOs interviewed, the signs of future
success were obvious well before the start of their business
career. For example, Robert Bandeen, formerly CEO of
Crown Life and before that Canadian National Railways,
started a business at age eleven on the family farm in western Ontario.

My sister and I started raising tobacco. We got a half
acre's rights, bought the plants, built a greenhouse. We
got up to ten acres. I think between us we would make
$12,000 to $15,000 clear. We had to rent barns to hang the
stuff in and we would have had up to one hundred
people working for us. At the ripe old age of fifteen I was
running these guys, paying them—the whole thing. We
had to get bank loans.

Of those CEOs interviewed, only 38 percent could be considered to have had a fairly affluent background, while 62
percent came from much less affluent beginnings. Coming
from a successful executive family is a mixed blessing. One
obvious advantage is that the children grow up with an
awareness of the business environment and a familiarity
with the people in it. They learn to be comfortable with the
senior business executives they encounter in their family's
social milieu. On the other hand, the family level of success
can be intimidating to some children. They may fear that
they cannot meet parental achievements and standards. In
more extreme cases this may lead children to seek out a
counterculture where the values and standards of the
home are rejected, thus freeing them of the need to
measure up. In other instances, the child may simply not
try. Sometimes success spurs children to demonstrate a
sense of independence. The slight, intense Louis Hollander, CEO of Canada Colors and Chemicals, discussed his
motivation. "When I got my master's degree, I said to my
father, 'That's it. You've helped me enough.' I wanted to

start from zero. That was a big motivator for me. Whatever I had I wanted to earn for myself."

Melvin Hawkrigg, CEO of Trilon, came from a blue-collar family of modest means. This stockily built man is an earthy, energetic person with a sharp-edged sense of humor.

> My father was a market gardener. During World War Two he worked on plant assembly lines. So I had no executive model. The rest of the family, uncles and aunts, were basically hard-working people in plants. Really, when I look back, my ending up in this position is unbelievable!

The preuniversity years are extremely important in the development of future executives. Our experience in assessing and counselling executives over the years has led us to conclude that there are certain values and influences common to the early lives of those who succeed. Our interviews with CEOs have confirmed these impressions, and indeed strengthened them. In simple terms, we have found that those who are successful have shared the following:

- Their families had a strong work ethic, which was accepted by the child.
- Their families loved, respected and encouraged them and gave them a feeling of self-worth.
- As children they were given a vision of what could be accomplished by effort. In the histories of CEOs we sampled, the direction was to business, but we are sure the same pattern of encouragement could be found with those who have excelled in areas such as the arts, education or politics.

These three characteristics were almost universal in the history of successful executives, and certainly in those at the CEO level.

Those who are successful tended to show early in their life a readiness to work hard (not necessarily at school), a sense of self-confidence and a feeling of competence.

One cannot predict that a child will emerge with a successful career from a positive environment since so many

factors, such as ability, affect the child's attitudes and opportunities, but those who are successful seem to have in
common an upbringing that stressed work, contribution
and achievement—the work ethic.

The energetic Lynton (Red) Wilson, CEO of Redpath Industries Limited, recalls that his father set the standard:

> From the time I was sixteen it was made clear by my father
> that I wasn't to sit around in the summers. So I went to
> work, and worked every summer right through until I
> finished university. In fact, like a lot of kids in those days, I
> paid my way through school by working in the summers.
> You could do that in a town like Port Colborne, where the
> wages were reasonably good and the work was there. You
> could put the money aside because you were living at
> home. It was something my father expected me to do. Had
> I ever needed money I am sure he would have provided it,
> but it was a challenge he set: make your way.

Robert Bandeen is tall and heavy-set and conveys vitality.
He remembers his mother's dictum:

> My mother's favorite statement was, "The devil makes
> work for idle hands." She felt if you were idle it was a sin.
> The whole Puritan work ethic.

In other cases, the home environment did not place direct
pressure on the child to achieve, but rather the influence
was provided by example. Working hard was simply the
thing to do. Gordon Farquhar, recently retired CEO of
Aetna Canada, grew up in such a family:

> It was performance by example. There was a very limited
> amount of verbal instruction, yet the standards were there.
> My father was extremely committed and dedicated to his
> community and the work he did, moving up through the
> ranks of a small mutual fire-insurance company to become
> its president. He showed me what one could achieve. He
> had great respect for the land, for family values and for
> doing things right.

As young people, these future CEOs found various outlets
for their drive to achieve. Yet the need to work or to excel

did not always find expression in the school environment. For some, it was dedication to sports or to social involvement with their peer group.

Michel Bélanger, CEO of the National Bank of Canada, recalls his school days, "I wasn't much of a participant in many things, but I was very active in Boy Scouts. I enjoyed making friends." Two years before he graduated he was elected class president and president of a literary society. He believes other factors helped him achieve popularity. "I was much taller than most of the other guys, which helped, and I fixed problems, which helped a few of my colleagues who the Father Superior had decided to throw out. I negotiated their integration back into school."

Alan Marchment, CEO of Guaranty Trust Company of Canada, was brought up in a family that celebrated effort. When he was a young teenager, Marchment took a *Liberty Magazine* route.

> No one encouraged me to take that on, but by sheer effort, I think, I developed the largest route in the area of the city I lived in. There were all the rewards you get from that, both money and coupons and prizes, but it was not something my parents encouraged me to do.

Like many of the CEOs we interviewed, Steven Wilgar, CEO of Warner-Lambert, participated in sports at an early age; he played football, hockey and golf in high school. Few of the CEOs were natural athletes, but the need to compete and, no doubt, to gain approval was evident in their teenage years. Lorne Lodge of IBM recalls he lacked the opportunity to play golf or tennis or learn how to ski as a student because his family didn't have a cottage and his parents weren't interested in individual sports. Yet he tried out for football, hockey and baseball in high school and university and made the teams. Many of the CEOs we talked to suggested that team sports gave them a sense of the importance of cooperation and leadership. Team sports also made them comfortable dealing with peers in a competitive situation.

The need to excel did not come naturally to all the CEOs we talked with; some needed a little encouragement to

direct their ability and attention to the activities and education necessary to achieve their later success. The majority
of those interviewed remembered that a parent or someone
else set an example and created the expectation that they
would do well. For some, the direction was by example,
but for others, it was more direct. Listen to what the
dynamic John Fraser of Federal Industries has to say about
a critical point in his life:

> My mother is a modest person who always gave me en-
> couragement. When I brought my marks home from
> school, Cs were considered fine and as a result I went
> through high school with so-so marks. Then, in grade
> eleven I went off the deep end and started to run around
> with a bunch of crazy guys, drinking beer and forming a
> union of students who tried to change the principal. At the
> end of the school year a friend and I took off to the U.S. We
> said we were going to be gone two weeks, but we were
> gone two months. At the time I really thought I was a big
> man on campus. I was on the football team and I had a
> great looking girlfriend. I was a good dancer and I wore
> saddle shoes. During the time we were away, the marks
> came in and I had failed my year. I came back expecting to
> go into fourth year and play on the first line of the basket-
> ball team and the first line of the football team. But Dad
> said, "Your marks came in. They're very bad. I got you a
> job." I said, "You what?" He said, "I got you a job with the
> CNR on a road gang." And I said, "No, I'm going back to
> school!" He replied, "No, I got you a job. Now we have to
> go downtown and buy you some work clothes." He took
> me down to a local department store, shrewd guy that he
> was, and bought me these big, heavy work boots. I had to
> take off my snappy little saddle shoes that I had just
> brought back from Los Angeles. I was with the "in" group,
> I was president of my class and that sort of jazz. I abhorred
> the work clothes and I sure as hell didn't want anything to
> do with that job. He said, "Come over here. Now look,
> you're going to work." I said, "Wait a minute, Dad, I'll
> make a deal." He thought for a moment and said, "All
> right, you can go back to school on one condition. The first

time you get a mark lower than A, it's over. And you have
to earn your own tuition and spending money. You can live
at home. We will keep you fed and dry and that's all." I
was consistently at the top in my class.

Growing up with the sense that work equals achievement
is only one factor. A child must also feel capable. CEOs
were not particularly aware of being made to feel capable
during childhood, but generally they were brought up in
homes where they were loved, respected and considered
worthwhile people. While being reared in a loving environment does not guarantee success, being brought up
with the feeling that you do not measure up to expectations is certainly an impediment. Confidence is extremely fragile. It does not take much to shake self-confidence or discourage us from doing what we set out to do.
As a group, CEOs, and indeed those on all levels of
management, have self confidence.

In our consulting and counselling work with managers
and executives, we have seen the devastating aspect of
growing up with a lowered sense of self-worth and power.
The symptoms—a lack of confidence and optimism, a
prevailing sense of a lack of worth—often betray people
throughout their careers. Feeling unwanted, or not as
valued as a brother or sister, some children fulfill the
prophecy and do not measure up to their parents' expectations. Such individuals often tend to live with the expectation of failure. Sometimes such an environment challenges the individual to overcome negative feelings, but
usually it results in a lack of confidence.

On the other hand, some CEOs, like Irving Ludmer of
Steinberg Inc., love a challenge:

I took engineering physics because I didn't know much
about careers, but I loved math and physics. Also I remember people would say, "Man, that course, stay away from
there, it's the hardest course there is and it's not the place to
go if you want to graduate!" That's like putting a red flag
in front of a bull, so that's where I was going to go. I
remember there were about fourteen of us who went
through all the years together; there were no other

volunteers. We had a couple of dropouts, but mostly it was
the same guys.

Two aspects of self-image are particularly important to
those who strive for the top. The first is a perception of
power and ability, the feeling that the person can do it,
whatever "it" happens to be. The second is the recognition
of the arena in which they wish to perform—be it business,
medicine, politics, or anything else. Many women, for example, view themselves as competent at a variety of activities—as mothers, teachers, volunteers and so on—but
they view the business world as alien. Someone who
visualizes himself first as a poet, will not likely be found
heading a company, nor will an individual who has never
visualized himself as a leader, even if that person possesses
the characteristics that lead to success in business.

While counselling young adults, we have found that the
family background often has a negative effect on goals and
goal setting. A number of years ago we were asked by a
client to speak to a young employee who the employer
thought had potential for advancement. When the position
was offered to the employee he turned it down. Puzzled by
this refusal, the employer thought that it was lack of confidence that motivated the young man to refuse the promotion. He also thought that being interviewed by a consultant might give the young man confidence. The interview
revealed that the employee had the ability to do the more
senior job. However, the young man, who was married
and had two young children, lived in a house located between those of both sets of parents. He was already more
successful than his father or father-in-law, and was uncomfortable at the idea of surpassing them further. He had
already achieved greater success than he had expected.
Since he was young, we thought the best thing to do was
to help him set higher goals for himself or to create a need
on his part to earn more. He was not a college graduate—
family finances and circumstances had dictated that—but
he wanted his two children to go to university. We pointed
out that with the income he could reasonably expect in his
present job, he would not have the money to send them to

university. He took the promotion, and we felt smug. A number of years later, we met the employer and asked him how it had all turned out. He said that it had not turned out well, and that the young man had left his employer a few years later. While we had succeeded in helping him see his real financial needs, we had done nothing to change his self-perception, his confidence or perhaps his ability.

Melvin Hawkrigg, CEO of Trilon, has a different story.

> My mother died when I was young. She had been a gentle, understanding person. The family split up after her death, and I was raised by two widowed aunts who each had two children. They were supportive, but not able to give me any sense of career direction. I had a high-school sweetheart from the age of sixteen and her father had a major impact on me. When it looked as if I would marry his daughter, which I did, he thought he ought to make something of me. He became my mentor. I had not been too bad a student in high school, but had not been motivated academically. After high school I had no plans. He encouraged me to go to university. I was approached by McMaster. I had no driving ambition, but it was a chance to play football. After graduating I had an interview with Westinghouse. I was told I had no skills and was advised to get a skill set so that I could bring something to the table. I had tied for top marks in an accounting course, and I was asked by a partner in Clarkson Gordon if I had an interest in getting a CA. I said no, but when I told my father-in-law he had a fit and I went to Clarkson Gordon. I qualified in 1956.

The story illustrates the importance of knowing what opportunities exist and grasping them. People from backgrounds that do not give them this vision have a handicap and at best may find themselves getting off to a slower start. For example, if family and friends are engaged in manual types of work, the individual may have only vague ideas about what else is possible. It may not be lack of confidence, ability or drive that constrains the person, but rather not knowing how and what to strive toward. It can then be a matter of luck, as it was with Mel Hawkrigg.

The fortunate individual is one who can find someone to help with information and goal setting. Then that person can get a good start on career building.

Some CEOs, like Lorne Lodge of IBM Canada Ltd., did it on their own.

> You must remember that nobody in my family had ever gone to university. While they were always very interested in my marks and my doing well at school, my family did not take it for granted that I would go to university or have any particular career. They had all been tradesmen. My father was a projectionist, my grandfather was a projectionist and all of my parents' associates were tradesmen. My parents didn't know anybody who had been to university. When it came time that I did want to go to university I found myself making phone calls to people who knew people who had gone to university—twice removed! I phoned them, introducing myself, telling them I was trying to decide what to take at university, and would they take time to give me some advice. I was surprised how much time a stranger would give on the phone to a person who was sincerely anxious for a little advice and counsel.

We live in a society where upward mobility is taken for granted. But those who are not fortunate enough, like Lorne Lodge, to find a mentor or adviser, may set their goals too low and underestimate their own ability. Later, of course, they may realize that their abilities were greater than they originally thought. This feeling of discontent frequently occurs in the late twenties or early thirties when it is much more difficult, though not impossible, to catch up with those who have high aspirations. In counseling, we often see individuals who thought they could achieve only a low level of work and had not acquired as much education as they were capable of absorbing and using. Many who went to work right out of high school or after a trades or secretarial course are in this category. After a while on the job, they realize that they could do as well as the person to whom they report. Many women who entered the work force when the range of work options was limited are in this position. Today, they still find impediments to the free development of their careers, but mostly they are held back because they did not develop the expectation that they could advance in their careers and they do not now know how to go about it.

Some may be lucky and find a mentor to encourage them, give good advice and help them find their way. For people who have not grown up in a business environment, the challenges, opportunities and means can be hidden.

The vast majority of the CEOs we interviewed had a college education, although some had obtained their degrees at night or after some work experience. As the challenges facing CEOs become more numerous and more complex, and with the number of people obtaining university degrees, it is not surprising to find a great number of CEOs with even two or three degrees. The important thing is, as Mel Hawkrigg discovered, to have a set of skills to bring to the table. Some kinds of training provide wider and greater opportunity than others. Those with trades skills may possibly advance in the manufacturing area, but will likely have difficulty moving into general management, where financial, marketing and communication skills are essential. But one fact is clear: exposure to education of any kind opens up new vistas and possibilities.

Robert Gratton, CEO of Montreal Trust, is a doctor's son. He was planning to attend the London School of Economics when a friend suggested he should be in business and go to the Harvard Business School. Gratton said:

> For the first time someone said, "You've got to plan this event." After that conversation I started to read about Harvard and a little about business, and what I read was that the Harvard Business School has a world reputation. So I decided to go to the London School of Economics for only a year and to apply to the Harvard Business School. Nothing could have been more foreign to me because I was anti-business during my years at university. I spent a year in London, got a master's degree in law, then I went to Harvard. That changed my life.

The families of most CEOs did encourage post secondary education; education was seen as the way for their children to have a better life. Charles Hantho, CEO of C-I-L Inc., recalled that his parents planned and saved to ensure that he could go to university. They even moved to South Mount Royal, a more affluent part of Calgary, to help their children.

> They wanted to put us in an environment where we were going to be exposed to kids who took it for granted that they were going on for further education. There was never a question of "Should I go to university?" It was expected that I'd go on to university, even though I didn't know that they were scrounging to put us through university. They wanted to make sure that I had the education my father didn't have. He recognized that to get ahead I had to get it, and they sacrificed to see that I did.

The decision as to what course to take was not always motivated by long-range planning. Alan Marchment, CEO of Guaranty Trust, recalls:

> I went to the University of Toronto. I started off in an arts course, and I took geology and actuarial science. I was en-rolled at Victoria College, and it turned out that I had taken no courses at the College, so I was called in and told I had to have two courses there. The only ones that fitted my timetable were philosophy and military studies, so I carried them that year. When I finished the year, I stood first in the university in geology, which made me think I should be-come a geological engineer, but while I was thinking about that, I was called in by the principal of the college. He said that I had been recommended by the head of the philosophy department to take the honors course. I told him I thought I would take geology. He said, "That's fine, but you'll have to start again, and that will be four years, but we'll let you into the second year of the honors philosophy course." Well, with the prospect of three years against four, I elected to go into philosophy, which I really never regretted.

Thomas Galt, the CEO of Sun Life Assurance Company, is tall, slim, reserved and very businesslike. He was a shy, quiet teenager who enjoyed mathematics, but had no

career in mind when he asked his high-school principal in
Arnprior, Ontario, "What can one do with mathematics?"
Galt explained:

> He said, "Well, you can teach," but I was shy, and teaching
> wasn't the thing I wanted to do. Because of my father, per-
> haps, I wanted to go into business. So he said, "Take math-
> ematics and economics and get a job as an actuary. When
> you get your fellowship you might make $5,000 a year." It
> sounded pretty good. All I could ever want.

Who were the most significant influences on these CEOs-to-
be? As one would expect, parents provided the major, but
not the exclusive influence on the development of early
work attitudes. Forty-five percent of the CEOs we interviewed mentioned their mother as being the most influen-
tial parent, 34 percent believed their father was the most
important and 16 percent felt the influence was equal. Five
percent found that some other individual was a more significant influence in their early years.

In speaking of his family influence, Trevor Eyton, CEO of
Brascan Ltd., recalled:

> My mother was the more demanding, more disciplined,
> more precise. I think that my desire to do well and achieve
> came from her. From my father I got what I consider the
> more important quality and that is the ability to enjoy
> things and to enjoy people, to preserve friendships.

Peter Gordon, retired CEO of Stelco, recalled that his
mother was a strong influence.

> My mother was probably more of an influence on me than
> my father. My father was an academic type, who graduated
> in classics from Acadia University back in 1900. He was a
> great reader, and he had a great understanding and feel for
> people. To have a son who was a mechanical engineer was
> probably the farthest thing from his mind. He worked for
> Imperial Oil and sold petroleum products, but that was a
> living for him. That provided food on the table for his
> family, so that he could do the things he wanted to do. My
> mother, on the other hand, was a hard-working, deter-

mined and loving individual, but the work had to be done first. My parents hired a maid. Even so, my mother would come down and dust the house and make sure the house was clean before the maid woke up! She made the soap. Nothing was wasted in the Gordon household while my mother was alive.

Ross Johnson spoke of his mother:

My mother started working when she was thirteen. She was a Scottish immigrant. She was a real driving force and had a hell of an influence on me. She worked herself up to be the assistant controller of the University of Manitoba. She was a major influence in that she was very power-conscious. She had very well-developed social skills. That included an understanding of the office. For example, when my father's boss's wife, who was older, had to go shopping, mother would drive her. And it worked. It helped my father tremendously.

For some, the influence of the father was limited because work kept him out of the home much of the time. Robert Martin, CEO of Consumers Gas Company Ltd., saw very little of his father.

A bread salesman's job was a tough go: it was a six-day-a-week job. I guess in that respect my mother was the major influence, although my dad was a very special guy to me. What he said was god-like. But I never saw very much of him.

Donald McIvor, formerly of Imperial Oil, had a great deal of respect for his father's intelligence, but felt his mother to be the driving force.

My mother had a hell of a lot of drive. If you needed spine stiffening she was the spine stiffener. She was the glue that made everything hang together.

Those who felt their father was the more powerful career influence spoke of his leadership, values and business success as having had an important part in their development. Many CEOs saw their fathers as standard-bearers—figures who had firm expectations of behavior, ethics and self-discipline.

"My father was the one who implicitly set the standards and discipline," said Lynton Wilson, CEO of Redpath Industries. "It was well-known that certain things were expected. Honor, truth, loyalty and determination. These were the values that were evident implicitly in the way he operated. He expected as much of other people."

The cordial Dean Muncaster, former CEO of Canadian Tire Corporation Ltd., says his father, a former Canadian Tire dealer himself, influenced him more than anyone else.

> One of several brothers who worked as a boy on a submarginal farm, he did not go beyond grade eight, yet he really understood people. I guess there are probably twenty-five or thirty Canadian Tire dealers who started as employees of his and thus came to him for counsel and advice. Early on, he instilled in me the idea that somebody had to lead things. He was extremely open about the operation of his business. He led me through his financial statements when I was twelve years of age.

Kevin Kavanagh of Great West Life Assurance Company also felt his father was a strong influence.

> My father, he's ninety now, was an Irish immigrant with a twist in that he had a degree in Greek and Latin. He arrived here in 1927 and laid tracks in the railway yard in Winnipeg when it was being built. Then he went to a country district to be a teacher in a one-room school with seven or eight grades. He ended up as a Latin teacher in the only high school in Brandon, and he taught grade ten, eleven and twelve Latin and geography to generations of kids. He was quite a guy. He wrote two books, one on La Vérendrye and the other a regional history of the Assiniboine Basin around Brandon. He was quite an influence on me, but bear in mind that I left Brandon after grade twelve and was back for only brief periods.

Other CEOs we interviewed said the influence of both parents was strong, but reflected different aspects of their lives. William Blundell of Canadian General Electric recalled:

> My father was a major influence through his example and questions. He was very honorable, very particular about paying debts and that kind of thing. Mother was more of a coach in that she did more counseling. I know it sounds a bit corny now, but they put tremendous emphasis upon responsibility to society. They were sterling examples of their generation. There was never much pressure put on me, but I was expected to do my best. When I went to university I tried to pay my way by working during the summer, but I needed a little help for board and room. At that time my parents made it clear that I had one try, and I had better put in a good performance at university.

Sometimes the influence of a relative was strong. In John Fraser's life it was his maternal grandmother.

> She had tremendous pride: she was a powerful, ambitious woman, much more so than her husband. She came to Saskatoon from the old country around 1910, got a job working in a restaurant, became a cook and ended up running the biggest, the best and the most successful university boarding house in Saskatoon. Her husband got arthritis in 1929. He was laid off and never worked again. My grandmother raised a huge family, seven kids. She was the only one in the family who was in business. During the war she bought and sold houses and bought land and grew potatoes and vegetables, which she used in her boarding house. She made all the kids work to help run the business. As the city grew she would sell some land and make some money. She ended up financially independent, not rich, but no one in the family had to take care of her. My drive and ambition came from my grandmother.

Through the influence of these people, these future CEOs developed attitudes and values that proved to be important in their later approach to work. Four main values seem to have been absorbed by those who have achieved the top jobs: hard work, high standards, integrity, contribution and leadership.

We have found CEOs, both in our sample of interviews and among those encountered over years of consulting, to be well-adjusted. They have good social skills and can get along with a wide variety of people: they have self-discipline and tend to be positive about themselves and others. The poorly adjusted and the unbalanced cannot make their way through organizations. They become frustrated by the need to work harmoniously with others, and their insecurities make it difficult for them to cope with challenges. The successful must, of course, be dedicated and serious about their work, but they need not be entirely single-minded or driven by some maladjustment, such as a fear of failure or a strong, competitive drive with a parent or sibling.

Success in any field of endeavor requires that a number of factors be right. Those who are successful in the corporate world had one personality trait that impressed us: they all had a positive attitude. Undoubtedly there is a tendency to recall the good parts of one's life and to forget the unpleasant, but we have come to believe that the generally happy recollections of those at the top are realistic. We did not hear many stories of rivalry with brothers and sisters or conflict with parents; rather the atmosphere of their early years was happy. Their backgrounds were often far from affluent, but there was not a lot of suffering either. The CEOs surveyed seem to have demonstrated a high level of social adjustment early in life.

To sum up: a good start does not necessarily lead to the top job, but those who do make it seem to have been well on their way by an early age. The critical factors are philosophical attitudes and examples set by the family, the love and respect received and a healthy sense of being capable and effective.

CHAPTER

3

MOVING
UP

M oving into the business world for the first time is no easy matter—in spite of how well one has been prepared in the family. Starting right lays the foundation for rapid advancement and new challenges in later years.

We explored this issue with all the CEOs we met and they affirmed that, to be successful, young people must pick entry jobs carefully. They must pick the right industry and company. To move ahead, to develop management skills, to become in time an executive means not just having picked the right place, but having the right plans, actions, attitudes and help.

There is no easy answer to the young entry-level employee who asks, "How do I get started on the right track to the top?" Not every job is for everyone. One's skills, interests and attitudes will influence where one starts, and where one starts can have profound influence on where one ends up.

For example, when we think of starting positions, we also think of line and staff jobs, so it is interesting to speculate on the question of if and how individuals in staff functions differ from those in line management positions. The question is a little fuzzier now than it used to be, since the terms "line" and "staff" are unpopular in some companies, and there is some movement to consider all positions to be "line." Nevertheless, there are some people in every organization who are charged primarily with either problem-solving aspects of the work or with responsibility for accomplishing a particular function. Observation suggests that it is unusual for someone in a specialized area, such as personnel or management-information systems, to reach the top job in a company.

Let us consider personnel managers. Observation and discussion with personnel executives often reveals that there is a great deal of frustration on the part of these managers because they feel they are not appreciated, and do not get a good hearing from management. Top management often seems to view the personnel executive as less likely to be promoted to the top job. Why is this the case?

Possibly, it is in part due to certain characteristics that differ significantly between personnel executives and top managers: the personnel types have lower economic values; less business interest; and are less interested in selling. They are, not surprisingly, more concerned with people; and they put more emphasis on being helpful. Finally, personnel executives have less interest in personally promoting themselves and their attributes. Thus the problem in communication and confidence often found between these two groups is not one of ability, so much as it is one of interest and attitude which causes a difference in outlook and emphasis that often makes the top manager uncomfortable.

The Right Place

To be successful, young people must be aware that entry-level jobs do matter and they must choose carefully. Where one starts could have a real effect on where one ends up. There are three aspects to consider: the industry, the company and the entry job.

On the whole, CEOs started their careers in industries that were healthy and had good growth prospects. A vibrant, successful and growing industry, such as the financial-services business, provides faster growth for those at junior levels and is more inclined to take chances on young employees by letting them try their ideas. When an industry is struggling for survival, the situation is just the opposite, and a junior manager or executive will have little opportunity to experiment, or indeed do anything but follow orders.

The executive or young manager can become less attractive to other companies if the industry he chooses to specialize in disappears. In general, the "smokestack" industries and a variety of other manufacturing industries do not have the potential found in a range of service and high-tech industries. Look for a healthy company; look for potential.

CEOs advise those who want to advance their careers to pick the most successful company within an industry. There are many reasons for this advice, not the least of which is that the leader in its field is more likely to need executives in the future. Moreover, since a good company is usually a sign of good management, the apprenticeship will be more beneficial. A healthy company is more likely to be able to afford the luxury of experimenting and taking chances, and to give younger managers freedom to gain an overall view of the business process. Thomas Galt, an actuary by profession and CEO of Sun Life Assurance, picked Sun Life because, as he explained, "It was the largest company in Canada whose presidents had always been actuaries and it seemed to me the opportunity there was greater than anywhere else."

A number of the CEOs we interviewed had their first experience in small organizations. They believe that involvement in a small organization allows a potential manager or executive to see the total picture and to understand the basic elements of buying, selling and making a profit. John Fraser, CEO of Federal Industries, worked as a part-time salesman for Jack Mallin's Menswear, a retailer in Saskatoon, while he attended university.

> He [Jack Mallin] was in his sixties when I started working
> for him. He was a shrewd and successful businessman.

Boy, did he like me, and I liked him. I learned more about business working for him after school that I learned in the College of Commerce at the university. He taught me to know my competition, to observe, to be organized and orderly.

Those who enter large companies as specialists in manufacturing, for example, may never have the opportunity to develop the broad view essential to general management. V.N. (Val) Stock, as a young employee at Canada Packers Inc., was a specialist, but broadened his experience by working for Chromalox Canada, a small electronics company. He became president of Chromalox and then moved to its parent company, Canadian Corporate Management Company Limited, where he became CEO. Later he moved again to Canada Packers, this time to become CEO. He said:

> If I had stayed at Canada Packers, I don't think I would have had the broad experience that is essential in running a large corporation. Problems are solved by specialists in large companies, whereas the boss has to be a generalist. Sometimes it's hard to find a good generalist, for instance, a person who has actually sat down and bargained or actually talked to the banks about financing. I think it is fair to say many of the larger corporations have a difficult task finding the right guy to fit the top job.

The philosophies of different companies create different environments for success; the individual who succeeds in one might not succeed in another. For example, Imperial Oil has a management-development system designed to identify employees with high potential. It is called a "top-down" management training system. Donald McIvor, former CEO of Imperial Oil Limited, described his involvement:

> The four organizational levels below me are where I spend my time. The presidents of the three operating companies and their vice presidents and my colleagues on the management committee. Their careers do take a lot of careful development.

David McCamus, CEO of Xerox Canada Inc., looks for four
things in potential management:

> Intelligence is the first thing I look for; second, integrity,
> people who are truly intellectually honest; third, people with
> a lot of initiative who are intelligent risk-takers who have the
> courage to go with their intellect and who are willing to put
> themselves forward and say, "I could be wrong, but I think
> we ought to do this," fourth, I look for interpersonal skills.

Some companies are more casual in their approach and, as
a consequence, the quiet but competent individual who is
not actively striving for advancement may be overlooked.
One philosophy is believed by many employees—if you
work hard and do a good job, you will be rewarded. This
may be nice, but it doesn't always result in recognition on
the job, since company managers are not all equally skilled
or disciplined in recognizing talent. One must take charge
of one's career rather than depend on the company.

Selecting the best functional area in which to begin a
career deserves more thought than it is usually given. We
found some major differences between individuals in different functional areas of business. Whether these differences were due to innate factors or to practice, we did not
determine. We do, however, think they are significant.

To make the comparisons, we drew from a data base of
more than three thousand individuals. We selected three
areas: production and manufacturing; finance and accounting; and marketing. We found that individuals in these
three areas differed significantly on fifty-seven of the
eighty-seven different measures. Those in production and
manufacturing were highest in:

- masculinity, particularly a strong physical approach
- the need for order and system, and a lower tolerance for
  ambiguity
- personal responsibility for attaining results
- the need to persevere and complete tasks
- an interest in theoretical or technical matters.

Not surprisingly, those in finance and accounting scored
significantly higher than those in the other groups on a test

of general problem-solving skills and in their interest in work involving numbers. However, those in marketing showed a significantly lower need for order than the other groups and exceeded both other groups in:

- understanding and dealing with others
- comprehension of successful sales techniques
- an interest in sales situations
- motivation for upward mobility
- self-acceptance or self-confidence
- an interest in activities that involve persuading others (for example, selling and negotiating)
- an interest in literary activities, such as reading and writing.

It is therefore not surprising that marketing executives have outdistanced executives from the other two functions in reaching the top job.

Surveys of company presidents in North America indicate the functional areas most likely to lead to the top. More presidents and top managers are being selected from the finance, accounting and marketing sections of their companies, and fewer from manufacturing and operations. As the business environment becomes more competitive, international and complicated, the financial and marketing strategies become more critical, and research and manufacturing aspects relatively less important, although there are significant differences between industries.

Ross Johnson, CEO of RJR Nabisco said: "The language of business is accounting, and if you don't understand the language, your chances of success are reduced." In filling senior positions, companies most often want general managers who understand the financial side and can read the numbers. Those who are weak in this area are likely to find that they don't make it to the corner office.

Marketing is also an excellent starting point because it provides an overview of all aspects of business. Law, while a less frequent entry position than finance or marketing, is still a major entry point, and is the only profession other than accounting that has a significant representation among CEOs.

Clearly, it is important for a young manager to avoid getting trapped in a narrow specialty that makes it hard to

have an understanding of the whole business. Bernard
Ghert of The Cadillac Fairview Corporation Limited told
us, "It's more important who you work with than what
you do. That's the real learning experience."

Jean de Grandpré, CEO of Bell Canada Enterprises, talks
about the importance of generalists.

> I think that to specialize people too early in life is not good
> in the sense that they have their nose to the grinding ma-
> chine too early in life, so that they haven't got the broad
> perspective that is so important. I'm not saying that you
> should not be good at a trade or a discipline: I'm saying
> that you should be the best in your discipline, but not to
> the exclusion of the rest. You should be good in written and
> oral communications. That's important in this world. You
> should have a non-discriminatory approach to issues be-
> cause if you are discriminatory in your approach, you're
> going to make the wrong decisions for the wrong reasons.
> You should have an understanding of political cross-cur-
> rents of this world; you should be exposed to issues that
> are not immediately related to your business.

The Right Plan
There is a fiction that those who have made it to the top
planned, created and seized their opportunities. Some of
these men did have long-term goals, others did not.

Kevin Kavanagh, CEO of Great-West Life, confessed:

> I really was doing each job as it came along. I never
> thought of being president: I wasn't overly impressed by
> my own ability. I thought I was capable in many respects,
> but not in every respect. My thinking had been to take each
> job as it came along and do my best in it.

But career advancement is seldom the result of luck alone.
We found that CEOs could be divided into two fairly distinct groups. The smaller group were those who always
aimed for the top job in any organization.

Discussing the motivation to get ahead, David Clark, the
enthusiastic CEO of Campbell Soup, confided, "If I joined
Cubs, I had to be sixer. If I went to a church group, I had to

be an officer. When I got into high school I was president of the student body. I was chief cadet, I was editor of the yearbook, and on and on."

Others were equally ambitious, but did not initially aim for the top. They tended to look ahead one step at a time and tried to excel at each position. For example, Bernard Ghert, CEO of Cadillac Fairview, said, "I never had any goals. I never planned a career. I just planned the work I was doing, planned how I was going to achieve my objectives in the particular job I was doing."

As far as we have observed, the difference between these two types of motivation had no discernible effect on the success of the individuals interviewed. We did, however, observe that those who made it to the top showed early signs of accomplishment in school, in sports or through leadership in a range of social, community or academic achievements. Even so, the drive to excel, to be a leader was apparent earlier in some individuals than in others.

Doing one's job well is one way to become visible. Good performance in turn leads to better assignments and the opportunity to show that you have what it takes. Taking on special assignments that concern senior management is another excellent way to bring oneself into contact with senior people. Donald McCarthy, now CEO of Beatrice Foods Ltd., was transferred to Nestlé Enterprises Ltd. head office in Toronto early in his career. After a few months the president, vice president and marketing vice president of the company decided they had many projects and jobs that needed administrative support. They created the job—staff assistant to management—and the first candidate was Donald McCarthy. "It was a fantastic learning experience. Working every day with the president and vice president, I learned how they thought, saw the projects they had and the pressures they were under."

Ways to gain visibility are sometimes built into the system. For example, good performance reviews often identify an individual for extra attention or special assignments. Sometimes, of course, a mentor or friend, or a senior person who admires an employee's performance may insure that a person is not overlooked. But these possibilities assume that an employee has done something unusual to merit attention in the first instance.

To insure the greatest opportunity for rapid advancement, the job environment should be approached in a way calculated to gain favorable attention. In his book *Managing*, Harold Geneen says, "You must play by the rules, going through the channels of the company structure, taking no short-cuts; but you don't have to think by the rules." Ross Johnson, of RJR Nabisco, describes this approach as "creative nonconformity." New ideas, new insights, new ways of doing things can gain one favorable attention. But unless innovation is within a range of familiarity, it may not be accepted by the organization. As Johnson says, you have to find out how the organization works, then adapt it to your own purposes. If you make everyone nervous about what you are doing, you won't win.

There is a strong rejection factor in every organization. When a new person seems to be making a mark, it is likely that some of the peer group, and possibly some in higher management, will feel threatened and may take some action to reduce the threat. For this reason, it is essential to have a strategy if one is to maintain fast, forward growth. David McCamus of Xerox Canada gave advice on this point.

> Never let a contest like that become overt; it has to be subtle. You can't lose your objectivity, and you can't do things that are out of character or that divert you from your goals. I have seen people win the battle but lose the war. I like to think I have done well because I don't get into the muck and mire. I do it by doing the job and not being personally vindictive. I never carry any scar tissue.

To achieve positive visibility takes a lot of work as well as some luck. The young manager must be aware of what is happening in the company. He must understand what the problems are and he must know the history and personality of the organization. He must introduce new but acceptable ideas. He must also be flexible and generous (but not to the point of self-effacement) in sharing credit. Many people attribute their success to being in the right place at the right time, but do not tell you how hard they worked to find out where the right place was and how hard they prepared to be there with the right stuff.

It is important to remember that what is good for the boss or for the company may not be good for the young manager. We have interviewed dozens of individuals at all levels of the corporate structure who have resigned from companies that refused them promotions or transfers they deemed necessary for career growth.

It is possible to become blocked in an organization for a variety of reasons. In some organizations everyone has to wait his or her turn, and there is no fast track. Perhaps the organization is very conservative and resists the prodding of an ambitious employee on the fast track. In times of management cut backs, takeovers and mergers, the career outlook for individuals can change drastically and quickly.

Ross Johnson, now of RJR Nabisco, has built his career by moving from one situation to another, seeking new experience and greater responsibility and challenge. His opinion is that when there is nothing more to learn or contribute one should move.

The Right Actions

All managers and executives have problems, and many of their subordinates are only too happy to bring them more. The subordinate who can solve problems is a joy and is likely to get ahead. The challenge is to find solutions others have not.

We believe there are four rules for getting ahead.

Do More Than Is Expected

The person who does more than is expected gains the attention and the gratitude of the superior (unless that superior is running scared and sees the subordinate as a threat). More important, doing more than is expected demonstrates motivation and a readiness and willingness to work. It also illustrates the fact that the employee sees beyond the specific job and has a wider idea of the company as a whole, and that the person has some of the characteristics of the generalist. A generalist, one whose skills or interests extend to several different fields, is highly prized in the corporation, assuming he or she has other attributes.

Most managers soon tire of the individual who does his or her job and no more. Reluctance to take on more than minimal work indicates a lack of ambition and may even show a certain meanness of spirit. An employee who takes the attitude "I'll take my money and run," is usually seen as uninterested in the job.

Seek Recognition

To gain recognition, the employee must understand what makes managers feel comfortable and confident. Managers are looking for assurance that what they want done will be done, and done well. If additional work is taken on and completed, it will make the subordinate stand out. Robert Hurlbut, CEO of General Foods, said, "When my bosses had new assignments or when new jobs were being created, I was the one who was ready to do them. I did it without blinking an eye."

To get ahead an employee should not only seek the recognition of the immediate boss, but also that of others highly placed in and outside the organization. Ross Johnson did this early in his career. As a young accountant he became involved in some new work: the computerization of some Canadian General Electric accounting functions. This task captured the attention of senior executives because it was new and potentially very important. By doing this job well, he gained the recognition of many important people in the company.

Gain Responsibility Early

The responsibility could be gained in school, extra-curricular activities and outside job interests as well as on the job itself. Such responsibility provides an opportunity to develop confidence in leading others, making presentations and other executive skills. It is also an early demonstration of one's ability, increasing the chances of being recognized as a "comer", and eligible for advancement.

In addition to having knowledge of their specific industry, successful executives also require a number of transferable skills that will enable them to move within the company or to another company. David McCamus, CEO of Xerox Canada, described the principle he adhered to when moving around in the corporate world.

> I tried to find an area quickly where I could make a contribution. Don't stay too long in the new-boy mode. Get yourself accredited as doing something significant. You've got to get some "value-added" quickly in the situation because there is a strong rejection instinct within any organization to anyone that's new. The second thing to do is adapt to the new company's culture. You can't expect them to adapt to yours; you've got to change.

Be A Creative Nonconformist

Creative nonconformity is essential. The person who does nothing unusual will soon become invisible. Yet there is a balance to be attained and maintained. It is necessary to gain recognition without upsetting too many people—or at least the wrong people. You have to stand out to be seen, and you need to be seen in the right way. The right way varies from company to company, but a few basics are probably universal.

The critical point is to be seen as the kind of person who has the boss's trust and respect. If one is perceived otherwise, the chances of getting ahead are very much reduced.

The Right Attitudes

What qualities does a superior look for in managers? There are a great many factors, and their importance changes with the times and the company, but there are a few that are universal.

Comfort

Any boss wants to be comfortable with a subordinate. No boss likes to worry about loyalty or about a subordinate's adherence to the ethical values and principles of the organization, whatever they happen to be; and no one wants a subordinate who causes more trouble than necessary in getting things done. Comfort with a subordinate comes from having confidence that the individual is competent, has good judgment, is reliable and can get things done without causing a negative groundswell. Someone who thinks, who challenges ideas and data and reacts essentially the way the boss does, provides this comfort. Someone who can also bring creative ideas is a jewel.

Competence

At the lower levels of some organizations, it may be difficult to determine who contributed what to an achievement, but at successively higher levels individual competence becomes more obvious.

Bosses look for two factors in particular. Most obvious is the subordinate's ability to identify and deal with the problems and opportunities presented—"to do the job." Individuals who have demonstrated this ability in a number of different roles will likely be perceived as competent. Second is the capacity "to take the heat"—to cope effectively with the physical and emotional stress the job entails, and to face and recover from mistakes in a constructive way. Many executives advised those who want to get ahead not to brood over errors, but rather to learn from them, fix them and get on with it.

Skill With People

At the early stages of a career one can get favorable attention by being technically good, by being a top engineer or accountant, for example. As one progresses up the organization, a higher level of competence is expected. At this stage the ability to get along with people and to get things done without undue fuss is a key to success. One CEO confidentially said to us that he could name eight or ten executives in the company with the intelligence and understanding of the industry to be CEOs, but only two had outstanding people skills. When all other executive skills are present, it is the level of interpersonal skill that makes the difference between the winners and those who "also ran."

Performance Now

Someone who gets things done will keep the boss happy, since the boss, after all, is looking for someone to simplify his or her life, not make it more complicated. Simplifying the boss's life means focusing on immediate tasks and finding answers that relate to broad corporate objectives, not one's own image or career. Immediate tasks must be tackled. Those who pervert this because of concerns about their career goals will usually be identified and found wanting.

The Right Help

When one reads profiles of successful business executives, celebrated scientists, lawyers, artists and politicians, three themes emerge. Their life stories may be quite different, but their rite of passage involved intense commitment to work, a clear vision of personal achievement and, for the lucky individuals at some point in their careers, the emergence of a mentor.

Classically, a mentor is selfless, courageous, loving and caring. The word has its root in Greek mythology. Mentor was a friend of Odysseus to whom Odysseus entrusted the education of his son, Telemachus. Today, a mentor is a trusted counselor or guide, a tutor or coach. In the work world, the mentor relationship might best be described as a warm and supportive bond between two people, in which the boundaries of position and self-interest are abandoned by the mentor, who has selected the protégé because of personal liking, or because the mentor believes the individual has potential worth developing. Sometimes it is as simple as a mirror image: "Jack reminds me of myself at that age..."

In the ideal relationship mentors foster their protégés' development by believing in them, sharing their dream, giving them their blessing and then setting out to help the protégés achieve their objectives.

Peter Gordon, retired CEO of Stelco, Inc. described his relationship with his predecessor, Harold Griffith:

> He had come up the same way I did. He chose me and the day I became president, he relaxed. He was in his early sixties when he gave me the job so I could learn it. Suddenly I found the loneliness of becoming the final fellow. But he helped bridge that gap, too, by acting as a father confessor and as a resource person. I had worked for him for twenty-five years. He is a father figure to me now, a very deep thoughtful fellow.

The bond between mentor and protégé must stand the test of time. Temporary setbacks or mistakes are accepted by both parties and the support given is mutual. Even if one partner leaves the company, the relationship, though less intense, often continues.

A mentor is a friend and teacher who is trusted completely, who will advise on tactics, timing and strategy, and who provides information and skill in coping with operational and functional tasks. Donald McGiverin, former CEO of the Hudson's Bay Company, reported that he was lucky to have mentors. He studied them, watching what they did and how they did it, observing their imagination, their ability to merchandise, to negotiate and to motivate.

A mentor is usually ten to fifteen years older than a protégé. When the age difference is less, the two are likely to view each other as peers. Peers may be friends socially, collaborating in a wide variety of activities, but the mentor aspect is likely to be minimal.

At times the mentor is an older family member. Melvin Hawkrigg, president and chief executive officer of Trilon Financial Corporation, describes his father-in-law as a key influence in his development as a young man by affecting his decision to attend university and by helping him choose his first employer.

In some cases the mentor's role broadens beyond the workplace and extends into the family and social life of the protégé. Acting as an impresario, the mentor may carefully orchestrate the development of important contacts for the younger person at business and social events. Some CEOs report meeting socially with their mentors beyond the confines of business.

Not all mentors assume an avuncular, supportive stance. When Louis Hollander left C-I-L and joined General Steel Wares as a divisional general manager of Beattie Bros., he focused on process (the handling of paper, factory scheduling and pricing inventory) rather than reducing overhead or changing the company structure. The division was losing money, but Hollander believed that by running the operation more efficiently without forcing change he could improve results. Hollander remembered:

> After a year, Ralph Barford, then CEO, asked to meet me over a beer. He said, "You're not going to make it. I don't see improvement." I said, "Look at all the things I've done." I had had ten solid years of successes. This had never happened to me before and I was mad. He really laid it on me and he was right. He helped me and probably has had more impact on my life than anyone else.

Not all relationships end successfully. Some so-called mentor relationships may be beneficial to the younger person, yet be seriously flawed because the underlying motivation is based on power, self-protection, even sexuality. The CEOs we interviewed reminded us of examples of mentors sponsoring talented young managers, but later, in fear of being eclipsed, behaving destructively at crucial moments in the protégés' careers. Ambitious executives in middle management frequently select one or two individuals who have demonstrated skills important to the executive's own success. The executive may help the juniors to broaden their scope of knowledge, as long as those efforts help make the so-called mentor look good. When there is no longer any advantage, the developing relationship is abandoned. One CEO told us of a long-term mentor who had hired him, then proceeded to guide him through the management ranks over a period of years, only to turn on him when he was getting too close and was thus a threat.

Even in their simplest forms, mentor relationships are complicated because they involve some degree of professional and psychological risk. Attitudes may change, trusted partners may become competitors, behavior may belie intention. The thoughtful young manager recognizes that while mentors may be helpful, the relationship is transitional and may possibly be marred in the end by resentment, anger or even grief. Whatever the motivation, important short-term advantages can develop that may enhance the career growth of the junior person as long as the mutually advantageous relationship is viewed realistically. Some large corporations have almost institutionalized the mentor relationship for promising executives by initiating management development systems designed to identify those employees with high potential and to ensure that they get the experience and exposure that will prepare them for the top jobs in the corporation. We do not believe, however, that mentors can be effectively institutionalized since one cannot order someone to take a genuine interest in another person.

While the majority of CEOs interviewed reported that they had a mentor, we noted that many of these people were not mentors as such but rather strong role models. There is an important distinction. A mentor is a wise and trusted counselor, but a role model may be neither wise nor trusted. A role model may simply display a particular talent, characteristic or type of behavior that a person seeks to emulate. The role model may not be a close colleague, or even be aware of his or her influence. The role model may be looked up to for a single quality, like a spectacular skill in sales. James Burns, CEO of Power Financial Corporation of Canada, recalled his role model:

> The Great-West [Life Assurance Company] manager was a fellow by the name of Earl Schwem and he was one of the top five life insurance people in the United States. He was a very highly regarded sales manager, and he certainly was a great influence on me. You couldn't stay around him very long before you got the perception of the dimensions and the size of the business, what could be done in it and the fun that there was in it. In those days, he would have been earning $250,000, which would probably have been about

what the chairman of General Motors was getting. He was a very successful, very smart, tough business man and a shrewd investor who made a lot of money. He had a lot of influence, because of his optimism and skill in sales.

Each of the CEOs we interviewed also recalled that there were many people without station or status (within the corporation) who served as important role models. Donald McCarthy spoke of his early career as a clerk in the traffic department at Nestlés. "I had the good fortune of having a very strong tutor in the traffic department, a lady named Mildred Murray, who really knew traffic management. She took me under her wing and taught me the business and was very helpful to me." Seventeen years later, McCarthy became president of Nestlé. "I had the opportunity to appoint that woman as traffic manager, because, in part for chauvinistic reasons, she had been overlooked all those years."

All the corporate leaders with whom we spoke adapted and learned from a wide range of individuals whose philosophy, skills and talents they could emulate. Ross Johnson, CEO of RJR Nabisco, spoke with near reverence of no less than three associates who influenced him. Johnson recalled:

> The general manager at General Electric showed me that the careful, patient approach pays off. He showed me that you get a report, you read it and then you look for other ways to accomplish the same result. He was a guy who said there were eight ways to solve things.

Johnson also tells the story of the late Tony Peskett, formerly at Eatons.

> He made me aware of the political maneuvering, and the handling of people. He could have been called a frustrated president. He showed that there are certain power spots in a corporation and that you can take any job and build it. If you get control, you don't have to be the boss, you run the place.

Johnson finally spoke of Ralph Barford, his boss at General Steel Wares.

He made me the businessman that I am. He showed me the
tough side of management. He had the energy, the drive,
the absolute total narrow focus and dedication that people
can get but that I had never realized. He was determined.

It is obvious that the role model can be as important as the
mentor and that having some form of a mentor
relationship can be a vital asset in the management climb,
but it is not essential. In our judgment, positive role
models are just as important to personal and career
development, and much easier to come by. Michael
Cornelissen of Royal Trust says he found that role models
in each organization he has been part of were individuals
who embodied particular qualities he admired and from
whom he learned values which have stood him in good
stead to this day.

The combination of luck and foresight that has brought
CEOs to the top job has included:

- picking good starting places for their careers;
- managing their own careers rather than taking whatever
  comes;
- insuring that they learned, grew, contributed, developed
  executive skills, and were recognized;
- developing attitudes and skills that increase effectiveness; and seeking
- wise counsel.

As the experiences of chief executive officers suggest,
career development is not a hit-or-miss matter. Whether a
young person aspires to the top job or not, the ability to
continue to move ahead, to take on new responsibilities
and challenges is very much the result of self-discipline,
dedication and a clear eye. Those who choose the right
place and develop the right plan have set a solid foundation. Advancement along the road to the top is more assured with a good foundation, coupled with the right actions, attitudes and help.

4

REACHING
THE TOP

O f those executives who eventually reach the top job a few make it by luck, some by unforeseen circumstances, most by solid dedication and preparation. What happens when the new CEO steps into the job? Is there a way to grasp the helm that sets the course for a successful run as leader of the organization?

When a new CEO walks into his office for the first time, he begins to sense very quickly that the whole nature of his life has changed dramatically. Robert Morison, now CEO of Consumers Packaging Inc., described how he felt when he became the CEO of Consumers Glass.

> You go through the euphoria of getting the job and all those things, and suddenly you realize, hey, this is a different job to what I thought it was. This is a lonely job. This is a job where you have to be very careful of what you say and to whom. It's a job where you are totally responsible, except that you can't specifically implement what you'd like to do because you've got to work through a whole bunch of people. So I found within six months to a year that the job

of CEO was totally different from anything I had conceived of. As an operating executive of the company, I had conceived of the job as directing these guys. It seemed easy. Suddenly, you get into the CEO slot, and you find out that no matter how much you know about the operating details or specifics, you have a whole bunch of guys working for you who are in charge of these things and you've got to let them have their time and their reign. Suddenly you are one step removed and your influence on the company has changed. You're no longer the guy on the line. Suddenly you find that you're there, and you can't do the things you used to.

Certainly these feelings of sudden shock and inadequacy have been experienced by many other CEOs. They suddenly sense that all eyes are on them. Lynton Wilson, CEO of Redpath Industries, remembered coming into his role:

> I guess in most organizations, especially with a guy coming in from the outside, the little things are very important to people. The signals that you inadvertently give. People are watching you much more closely than you think for those signals. They want to know how the new guy handles situations, they want to be able to predict what he is going to do. All the little signals are very important. How formal and informal are you? What kind of access you give people to you? People are watching to see exactly how to respond, how you deal with situations, how angry you get, what kind of rewards you give. They want to know where they fit, what their job is and whether they are doing well. They look for all the signals that tell them that.

The late Val Stock emphasized the importance of setting an example.

> Simple things, like I was always the first in in the morning. I was always the last out at night. I never demanded anything from anyone I wouldn't have asked from myself. I always said if you are going to work with the people you might as well be an example rather than just say "Do it my way," and then do all these other things. I think that has been a strength, because if you do that, people tend to

respond to what you are talking about. If you are going to get tough they don't mind you getting tough because you are equally as tough on yourself. I rode a subway downtown. I didn't have a chauffeur-driven limousine. People noticed that, you know. I answered my own telephone. They all noticed that.

Let's examine some of the concerns of new CEOs.

First is the new chief executive officer's realization that he is the ultimate conflict resolver. The very nature of his organization is such that the heads of all major activities report to him and that every decision that crosses activity lines, every trade-off and every conflict between areas requires his involvement.

Second is the realization that few important issues can be delegated. Since most issues do not fit neatly into a particular functional area, they cannot be handed over to a strong lieutenant. As the key integrator in the organization, the new CEO spends his days dealing with "issues management" as distinct from "functional management."

Kevin Kavanagh, CEO of Great-West Life, emphasized issues:

> Take this issue: There's a whole big opportunity out there in terms of the accumulation of wealth and I think that in the last ten or fifteen years middle-class people have started to have assets that I don't think the middle class had twenty-five years ago. And I think that's a real issue to turn into opportunity for us. Let's figure out how to do it.

In addition, the new CEO realizes how important the outside world of the company is. Forces of change in the marketplace directly affect the operations of the company and yet the new organizational leader has little control over them. More distressing is the realization the earlier functional experience and teamwork have ill-prepared the new CEO for handling these new publics. James Burns, looking back to when he was CEO of Great-West Life, said, "The gap is enormous. It takes a few years to find your way around, then three or four to really get things in motion: your business plan and your ambition for the company."

Our experience suggests that the new organizational leader's early actions will set his future leadership style and determine his ability to motivate others to perform well. New CEOs who do not succeed in motivating others, who, at best, continue in a business-as-usual way, have consciously or unconsciously let structure take contol of them, rather than taking control of the structure.

Ross Johnson of RJR Nabisco has some views on such CEOs:

> How self-sufficient does a chief executive have to be? He's got to be able to do his own work when he has to. He's got to take up the goddamned pen and push paper. The problem is when some executives get there they don't know how to act the president. They don't know how to be the president. I've watched people. Their whole thing was to become the president, and when they hit it, they couldn't handle it. They are either too soft or too hard or they quit using the skills that got them there and start wasting time on other things.

That is a far cry from a former leader of a major Canadian public company who held his position for more than a decade (and whose performance is quite forgettable) and who told us that his means of coping with the new, complex realities of his role was to "allow the structure to take hold." In fact, from his first day on the new job, there was a tacit understanding that key support staff were there to guide and nurture him (as they had done for his predecessor). He said quite frankly (and proudly) that the organization was so strong that any one of the other functional heads could just as easily have been placed in the role and succeeded because of the "marvelous" support structure.

Other CEOs who fail to leave their mark are those who, rather than face the issues they must cope with, spend their time doing what they know (and like) best. As a consequence, they direct much of their energy to the functional area they came from. The former chief financial officer spends hours poring over financial statements and then sends out more demands for new variance reports. The former head of marketing begins thinking about specific new marketing tactics and starts to go out on the customer circuit. The former head of production is seen touring the plants too often. In the meantime, the paper piles up, the files grow thicker and those waiting for inter-functional issues to be resolved and priorities to be set grow more impatient and concerned.

Not surprisingly, major public companies that are highly structured rarely fail because the new chief executive officer does not change his attitude from his previous job. Highly structured organizations, such as the functionally oriented ones, generate a certain momentum over time. They become true bureaucracies, churning out predictable and usually reasonable, if not substantial, annual revenues and profits, regardless of the style of leadership from the top.

As the years pass, each major functional area becomes a solitude—independent, insular and, in time, inbred. Little informal communication runs between functions because, since reporting relationships needed to be protected, for-mal linkages are religiously adhered to. Staff support positions are added over time to give assistance to existing staff positions (or to justify another grade or level in the formal salary system).

Indeed, one finds in too many instances that these care-fully formulated compensation systems become too dominant a factor in the evolution of the structure of the organization. They are arrived at by a mathematical for-mula, and most require job evaluations. Therefore, descrip-tions of a position are often written to gain "points" for salary purposes rather than to describe the function, authority, accountability and standards of performance that are the true elements of management.

If more points are given to those who manage more people, then one has to find a way of adding some people to one's group. If more points are given to those at higher levels, then one has to find a way to describe one's current duties in a more magnificent manner. Worst of all, highly skilled professionals and specialists who simply want to concentrate on their area of excellence find themselves taking on undesired administrative and supervisory responsibilities because it is impossible to move up the salary curve without taking on such duties.

In organizations of this nature the annual salary adjustments of senior supervisors, managers and executives are dictated by the formula of the compensation system—always standard, always predictable and nearly always bearing little on any effective measure of the real performance of each individual.

Thus, the compensation system adds to the inertia of the large, highly structured corporation, as do its rigidly adhered-to budgeting systems and its policies and procedures for job change and promotion—in fact, its conformity to standards for just about everything in a working day. What happens? Not much. This inertia will overtake even the man in the chief executive's corner office if he does not take charge of his organization. Each function becomes an independent empire, which can, to a large degree, survive by itself for a long time. But the whole, the quality of the corporation, will inevitably suffer as a result.

But what of the chief executive officer who recognizes the problems and wants to deal with them and create a different, less functional and more interactive environment? What is it that he does differently?

Our observations suggest that his first step is to accept the fact that he is going to have to work far harder than he expected and harder than most, if not all, of those around him. As Harold Geneen so aptly put it in *Managing*: "Your working days belong to others." The leader who devotes his working days to others—to those in his own organization and the many diverse people who purchase its products or services—has to find additional time, those hours before others begin their day or after most have left. These hours are his time to think, to plan, to study, to work out quietly the decisions only the chief executive officer can make.

Three CEOs talked about this precious time. Robert Gratton, the young CEO of Montreal Trust:

> "They said all over the place that I was a workaholic. Of course, I don't like working, but to do what we have done here requires a lot of work and I have to keep the pressure

on. I tend to be a perfectionist. I get into something because it is important, or because it's not in good shape. I worked hard and put a lot of pressure on myself."

William Blundell, the CEO of Canadian General Electric:

> One of the things I did learn early is the best way to avoid stress and a heart attack is to have your homework done. I'd rather go home and work on the weekend and come in Monday and be prepared than not work on the weekend and come in Monday and try to sort it all out.

Richard Thomson, the head of the Toronto-Dominion Bank:

> The single thing you've got to keep to do a CEO's job is freedom; you've got to have that freedom to allocate your time, because you don't know what tomorow's problems are going to be.

One change a new CEO can make is to develop the sense of teamwork. Over the years the heads of departments often become isolated from each other and tend to go directly to the CEO for a resolution of an interdepartmental problem. In this way they sometimes create small empires around their function. This situation leaves the CEO as the only one thinking and worrying about the company as a whole. The new leader who intends to create a changed atmosphere usually recognizes that although a formal structure and a chain of command are necessary, it is also essential to break down the solitudes and turn the function heads into managers who communicate with each other and form an integrated team. He recognizes that the structure is just a series of boxes on paper joined by lines—full or dotted. Even when one adds people one only has names at the bottom of the boxes. In order to make the organization come alive, the individuals must be brought together to function as a team and to think as one about the directions and goals set out by the chief executive officer.

By doing so, the chief executive officer achieves three things. First, the specialized knowledge of key management is pooled and can be used to solve issues requiring interfunctional skills. Second, a new environment is created in the organization, which in time will help to give his key subordinates an understanding of and exposure to company-wide issues. Third, the organization becomes an extension of the CEO's decision-making process and preferred style, rather than the reverse.

Robert Gratton described his introduction to Montreal Trust:

> I got the board to agree to my joining Montreal Trust as a consultant. Everybody had been told that I would be the next CEO. Meanwhile, I sat in this office with this table for two months and I interviewed everybody. I made notes of every interview, reviewed them at night, worked very hard at it, very systematically. I did the same thing with the department heads in the branches. I went across the country, and after two months I had a thick book. It increased my knowledge of the inside of the company so that by the time I became CEO in April I was in position, at my first executive committee, to say, well, this is what I want to do for the next year or so. I had a plan that was rooted in some knowledge of the company.

Successful CEOs have also gradually reshaped their organization's structure, causing a full or partial breakdown of the traditional, functional, centralized structure in the lower ranks of the organization. Efforts have, in some instances, been directed to moving authority further down into the organization—to push conflict resolution as far down as one can without abdicating key decision-making responsiblity. The evolution toward the concept of business units or small profit centers has helped achieve this. In addition, such moves have led to building a new generation of general management skills over time. These people are far less functionally rigid than those referred to earlier. The new, young chief executive officers are often the beneficiaries of having had this early general management exposure. They should be grateful to their predecessors, who dedicated the tremendous time, energy and devotion necessary to gain control over their structures—leaving their mark of excellence.

As well as reshaping the structure, the new CEO can use his talent to vitalize an organization and to motivate employees. Most CEOs recognize that it is they who shape the company, not the company that shapes them. Alan Marchment, CEO of Guaranty Trust, said:

> I would say that I shape the company. I think that's what a CEO has to do. Someone has to have a vision. Someone has to give leadership, and you can't pass that down to anyone else.

Bernard Ghert, CEO of Cadillac Fairview has a different view.

> In some ways I shape the company; in some ways the company shapes me. I have to behave in certain ways because of the business we're in.

John Fraser, CEO of Federal Industries, has no doubts on the subject.

> When I take over as a head of a company, it becomes my company. It's a reflection of me, it doesn't really alter me a hell of a lot.

And, as a final note, those CEOs who have grasped the helm recognize the significance of the position. Ross Johson, CEO of RJR Nabisco, summed it up:

> At the time I became chief executive officer I began to recognize that the job was bigger than me in terms of recognition. There was a halo effect around my name that I really hadn't appreciated in the past. It's amazing the power that the position carries with it.

2

LEADERSHIP

Leadership makes the difference, it is what differentiates the successful organization from the mediocre. It is what distinguishes the truly effective chief executive officer from the mediocre. Leadership is an amalgam of qualities, traits and values coupled with certain skills. In this section we explore these, as well as the personal cost of leadership.

C H A P T E R

5

LEADERSHIP

At one point in his career, Robert Martin, now CEO of Consumers' Gas, was in charge of the company's operations in the Niagara Peninsula. He was faced with a major labor dispute, which appeared to be moving quickly into a strike situation. This was a shock to Consumers' Gas, for it had never had to deal with a strike in its history. There was no book, no set of rules for Martin to follow. Martin knew the union wanted a strike no matter what happened.

> There was a team of about forty-five managers down there and I called these guys together. I told them that despite the fact that I would continue to negotiate as long as I could, it was my conclusion that there was going to be a strike. I said that our responsibility together was to keep the company running. I guess I gave them a little Knute Rockne. I had never been in a strike. We were really going to be tested to see what we were made of. I looked for their loyalty and support. I got it. I involved them all in planning just how we would operate and what we hoped to achieve. When the whistle blew and the guys walked out, we were

ready. Those forty-five managers had their chests out and
they were going to run the goddamn company, and they
did. For three months. And never, never a question. Guys
worked seven days a week. It taught me a whole lot about
leadership. You can't drive people to do things that are un-
natural. But you can get people to support your cause if the
cause is there, and if they are part of it.

Martin's story is not necessarily the stuff of high drama.
Yet his call for dedicated cooperation and his follow-
through in what was a dramatically new encounter ex-
emplify many of the basic qualities of leadership.

Leadership is what the capable CEO is all about. The
chief executive officer is responsible for ensuring that the
corporation produces goods and services in a manner that
efficiently meets the demands of the marketplace. As the
previous chapters have shown, he is the principal communication link between the corporation and its public,
and he must be sure that the organization serves the goals
of those who own it. But at the same time the CEO must be
an activist, a spokesman and a diplomat. It is his job to
define corporate vision—to let people know what business
the company is in, where it wants to go and how it's going
to get there. It is his job to make it happen. And it is his job
to maintain an impeccable corporate image within the
community.

This is a pretty tall order for anyone, especially when
you consider the complexities of the issues the CEO faces.
He operates in a wide world of international trade, in an
advanced and varied business, with increasingly advanced
technologies in an unpredictable environment. It all adds
up to the fact that the CEO has less time to run the operational affairs of the business. He must be more a leader
than a manager, more a generalist than a specialist. He has
to be able to develop strategy; he has to inspire; he must
lead.

Leadership is perhaps the most difficult attribute to
describe. Rowland Frazee, former CEO of the Royal Bank of
Canada, believes this elusive quality simply cannot be
taught:

A person is born with it, or in the very early stages of their lives, their environment puts them in a position, somehow or other, whereby they can exhibit some leadership. It is something that is instinctive and can't be taught. If you sent someone to me today and said make a leader out of that person, I couldn't do it. I could make a manager out of him, but leadership is just something that's almost impossible to define.

Of all the definitions of leadership, we believe Crawford H. Greenwalt summed it up best when he pointed out that the most important function of a CEO is "to reconcile, to coordinate, to compromise and to appraise the various viewpoints and talents under his direction and [see to it] that each individual contributes full measure to the business at hand." That's leadership and it is not limited to the top job. Everyone who manages people has the same opportunity.

In our view, leadership is a curious and rather remarkable amalgam of personal abilities, traits, values and differing sorts of power that are combined with skills that may be developed by anyone who has the commitment and capacity to learn. We believe there are several qualities shared by all the individuals who reached the top. None of the CEOs we interviewed could offer an instant list of leadership qualities. Most of them thought carefully and offered a few suggestions they thought were important in assessing leadership in others. At the top of their list (although expressed in different ways) was _concern_—concern for people, about events and follow-through, about the competitive environment and about performance. When assessing the leadership potential of their employees, they did not look for individuals who worried or who were anxious; instead they looked for employees who were able to eliminate or relieve problems and who would then monitor the results and reactions—and take responsibility for their decisions. Melvin Hawkrigg, the CEO of Trilon Financial Corporation, put it simply:

If there is anything I have learned it is that the people side is so terribly important. You have to work with people and have them understand what it is that you want them to do and how you measure their performance and success. It's the importance of being able to know your people and understand your people.

Hawkrigg remembered his days as a leader at the Fuller Brush Company:

> The Fuller Brush salespeople were normal, every-day people who had never been recognized for any achievement in their lives. All of a sudden they came into a direct sales organization, and if they met their objective for the month or the week or the campaign, you would call these people up [at a sales meeting] and say, "You were absolutely tremendous. You just sold this and you led the way." You wouldn't have to give them a hell of a lot, but you would give something. There were numerous examples of individuals who, because of recognition and support, altered their self-image dramatically, as well as their performance. One who comes to mind is Tom. When he first came in, plain old Tom really didn't have much confidence. Then, by God, six months later, after you had given him all the training and the motivation, all of a sudden Tom was looking super and he had got himself a top performance and you'd bring him up to the mike. That's when it was really great. That's when you could take a hell of a lot of pride in having taken somebody who had no great expectations for himself or herself and then all of a sudden they'd made it.

The second characteristic or quality of leadership is the capacity of using *power with care*. There is no question that the position of CEO carries with it certain powers. Power to control information, power to control the allocation of resources, power to make things happen. Probably, along with these powers of the position, the incumbent brings certain personally developed powers. One may be a charismatic personality; another might have a clearly recognized and respected expertise. We have found that those who flaunt these powers, particularly those of the position, are rarely admired as leaders. Those CEOs who use them with care usually gain more lasting respect.

Trevor Eyton, CEO of Brascan, comments on the power of the position.

> I don't feel powerful and I don't really think that's the way we operate. We have great access here. I can see almost anybody is this country on short notice and talk to them, but I've never felt just because I asked them to do something that they had to do it. I've always felt that unless there are compelling reasons, legitimate and logical reasons, it wouldn't get done; and I think that's the kind of power everybody has, so I don't see that we're unique. I think power is so fragmented in this country that it would be very hard for anybody to say, yeah, I'm powerful. He may have the right to fire some poor guy in inventory or something like that, but that's not real power. I don't think any really healthy person looks for that kind of power.

Effective CEOs demonstrate above-average intelligence, but they are rarely intellectuals. Few of them could be classified as deep thinkers. Yet their capacity to absorb and retain essential information indicates they have great *cognitive skills*.

CEOs spend their days in meetings, and the range of information they must process mentally is enormous. The typical CEO attends an average of seven meetings per day, and almost without exception the people who meet with him ask for support. It may be a major acquisition or the closing of a production line, each involving millions of dollars and affecting scores of people. The CEO must constantly interpret and analyze information, and foresee the implications of each decision he is called upon to make. The ability to solve abstract and complex problems is essential for the CEO and, for that matter, for any manager.

Running five to eight meetings that often span ten to twelve hours a day requires *a high degree of energy*. Indeed, among the CEOs we met there seemed to be a passion for constant activity, whether within the company or through membership in associations, directorships or involvement in community affairs. All the CEOs attack tasks and problems with intensity and focus that belie the fact that many of them regularly put in twelve-hour days. All of them travel a great deal and, without exception, they use free time on aircraft to read reports or write memos. Work brings them a sense of worth and value, and their energy seems to flow from this fact. Although many of the men we met were in their fifties and early sixties, they all appeared to be fit, probably because the majority are involved in exercise programs.

A fifth personality trait we noted among CEOs was a *positive self-image*. They seemed to have the ability to recognize and appreciate their strengths as individuals and as businessmen. They also appeared to be comfortable with their limitations and offered to discuss their self-perceived areas of weakness with surprising candor. Michel Bélanger of the National Bank of Canada discussed skills of future managers in banking: "More people in senior management will have to develop the ability to understand technological change and appreciate its implications. I don't have the basic background to even realize where the next development could come." This is honest self-appraisal from a man whose breadth of experience spans the complex worlds of the public and private sectors.

This trait is probably linked to the fact that our CEOs have *little self-doubt*. They spend little time analyzing something they've said or done that didn't work out as intended. Ross Johnson, of RJR Nabisco, claims he doesn't waste time worrying about an event that is history, even if it occurred that afternoon. If the words did not come out right at a presentation or a board meeting, for example, Johnson said:

> I'll feel badly, but what I'll do is concentrate on improving. I'll go over it in my mind so I'll be ready next time. That's what's important—tomorrow.

Johnson believes people are too hard on themselves:

> You can't set goals that are unreachable, but you can say, "Look, I can make it better." Maybe someone else could make it much better, but at least you tried. It's important in life to recognize that there will always be someone else who is better looking, or who can jump higher than you. If

you're going to be happy in any job, you should set high but reasonable standards.

Perhaps this attitude is responsible for a widely held sense of *optimism*. Although they may dwell on their problems in private, we found CEOs to be positive thinkers, at least in the company of others. They try to eliminate negative views, and they have little respect for managers who focus on problems. Maurice Jodoin, CEO of General Trust, isn't embarrassed to tell people that Dale Carnegie was right: there is power in positive thinking. "A successful manager needs to think positively—it's a very important quality. You can do whatever you want if you really put your mind to it."

David McCamus, head of Xerox, talked about inculcating optimism into the organization.

> I have an approach I call "success management". We are successful, therefore, we must know a lot about success. Everybody comes to a company wanting to be successful. So, you've got to institutionalize success. You've got to make it the norm. People around here are successful. There is a process associated with that. Do people understand those things? Are they trying to discover all over again, for the nth time, that you don't do that or you do this to be successful?
>
> So I have four principles of success management. Number one: select the best people you possibly can. Number two: train and develop them into successful people. Number three: combine motivation and discipline. The two go hand in hand; you can't separate one from the other. Number four: ownership. This comes when you finally get people who have accepted that it's their responsibility to do all this. It isn't you that has to be brought in every five minutes and bang the bird cage.

John Fraser of Federal Industries used a phrase that reflects another personal quality we attach to leadership ability—*natural curiosity*. "If you don't inspect, then don't expect," is Fraser's maxim. The only way any manager, including a CEO, can be on top of the job is by knowing what is going on in key operations within the company, and this doesn't

happen by simply taking a tour of a department or plant. It
means that the manager must ask questions, one form of
inspection, and observe with care. Our CEOs did not need
formal professional development any longer, but they all
showed great interest in new technology as it affected
company operations in the plant or office. Michael Cornelissen of Royal Trust emphasized the hands-on approach, insisting that successful executives cannot afford to
get themselves trapped in an ivory tower. He believes that
unless they force themselves to work in a non-manage-
ment capacity at various points in the organization to get a
feel for what is going on, they will lose touch with their
customers and never understand the real problems faced
by their field people.

If there is one quality essential to leadership it is *communication skill*. The CEOs identified this ability as a
primary need for their job and a central consideration in
promotion of managers. Although they didn't speak with
the eloquence of Roman senators, the fifty CEOs to whom
we talked expressed thoughts and attitudes clearly and
frankly. Since 90 percent of their tasks involves sharing
ideas and advancing concepts, they obviously need to
communicate effectively. Oral fluency is also high on the
list of qualities CEOs expect from their management ranks.
Robert Hurlbut, retired CEO of General Foods, suggests
that lack of communication skills can limit a manager's
progress, regardless of other skills.

> I have seen some brilliant people, high performers, fall flat
> on their faces, or fail to reach the top because they have
> been unable to communicate with people. That would be
> near the top of my list of criteria.

Since the content of the message is certainly as important
as the skill to deliver it well, the effective CEO should be
able to communicate a *compelling vision* to employees, to
shareholders and to the board of directors. Vision, or at
least the perception that the CEO has it, is especially necessary at a time when the business community is undergoing
turbulent change. He has the responsibility to communicate a clear sense of direction and thus inspire confidence

and enthusiasm. Most importantly, he should be able to generate commitment in those around him. The CEO or the manager who communicates with enthusiasm and relates the importance of the tasks to be completed will improve standards. The conviction that the task has value and is important adds to the likelihood of high levels of performance. Communicating with enthusiasm is a decided characteristic of excellent CEOs.

David McCamus of Xerox talked about a clear vision and what it takes to be a successful leader.

> It requires consistency. The secrets to success in management are having clear objectives and a consistent approach to meeting those objectives. Obviously, it has to be a methodology that works.

Gerald Hobbs, former leader of Cominco Ltd., commented wryly:

> You have to engage in theatrics, and they can be fun if you take them as a game. If you take them seriously and see yourself as the main character, then you're really getting askew of reality.

In any large company there are hundreds, often thousands, of employees who, from their more limited working environment, have concerns about the stability of their company. These people read, watch and listen. In the thousands of interviews we have conducted in organizations over nearly thirty years, we have never failed to be impressed by the fact that employees at all levels are aware of general trends and conditions in their industry. Regardless of conditions, all employees look for stability, security and a clear sense of direction in their organizations. They want to have confidence in their CEO. And they want assurance that the leader knows the right direction, that he has vision. David McCamus learned that lesson in university when he was elected president of his fraternity.

> These were all my buddies and I thought of myself as a kind of den mother. Finally, somebody came up to me and

said, "McCamus, we elected you because we want you to lead." I thought I'd simply annoy my friends if I did. When you take on the trappings of office, people want you to lead—spiritually and intellectually.

Yet CEOs are not dreamers. They *seize opportunities quickly* on a corporate and personal level; they deal with the moment; they focus on what they do and they don't spend much time on reflection. This supports the contention that leaders in any field have an agenda and an unparalleled concern for results.

When tough decisions have to be made, the CEO is looked upon as the heartless leader who doesn't care about people, loyalty or, in some cases, integrity. Many of the men we interviewed had made tough decisions and no doubt knew that their values were in question. Steinberg's CEO Irving Ludmer said:

> I tell people I like to play fair, as fair as the other guy is going to play. I give them a very unfair analogy: when the British were teaching everybody the Marquis of Queensberry rules for boxing, they were also breeding pit bull terriers. Sometimes you need the Marquis of Queensberry and sometimes you need that pit bull terrier. The streets are, in my opinion, an important part of my nature. I basically believe that nothing is going to come easily. You've got to work your you-know-what off, and there are guys working out there who would like to take a chunk out of you, so we had better have a few pit bull terriers in our place. You've got to be a scrapper and you've got to be a worker. It's not going to come by being laid back, showing up at nine o'clock, hanging up your degrees and talking very nicely to everyone—you've got to get after it. You've got to hustle because, believe me, the world existed before Irving Ludmer and it's going to exist after Irving Ludmer.

Yet, our sample indicated that these men did have a *genuine commitment to people* in their organization. Robert DeMone, the former CEO of Maple Leaf Mills Limited and now CEO of Canadian Pacific Hotels Limited, summed up:

I'm not managing a business, I'm managing people. I still couldn't run a flour mill if my life depended on it, or any of the other operations we have. I am helpless without people and I tell them that all the time. I tell them how important they are and how I couldn't do their job, but together we have a job to do. The results you can get from motivating people are mind-boggling.

One trait all CEOs share is *enthusiasm*. The fact that on average they put in a twelve-hour day, five days a week, and devote time on weekends to business tasks is in part due to the fact that they thrive on work. Most of our interviews with CEOs started slowly with the usual pleasantries. But once they relaxed, they became openly enthusiastic about describing their jobs and passionate about expressing their views. Their attitude is: if you have to spend so much time working, why not have fun at it? On the practical side, such enthusiasm leads to commitment and hard work. If a leader conveys enthusiasm, that's half the battle. That's what builds the team.

John Fraser, the dynamic leader of Federal Industries, said:

I love business. It's my hobby as well as my job. When I go away, do you know what I take with me? Business books. I love reading about business. I can get a real charge from reading about Iaccoca being brilliant or somebody else being dumb and trying to understand their strategy. I could sit down with any businessman and talk. If he wanted to open up to me about his business I would be just as fascinated in his business as I would be in my own.

Trevor Eyton, the leader of Brascan, echoed this enthusiasm:

I say it's fun, I just really enjoy it. I like the challenge and I must say I've always been a presser in the sense that if something seemed difficult I tended to try to do it. I like the feeling of getting up in the morning and being a bit nervous about what lies ahead that day, and then doing what I can to try to respond, to try managing it if I can. It is really trying to demonstrate that you can beat the inadequacies you feel within yourself, that you can measure up and you can perform.

When asked why he was so enthusiastic Bernard Ghert, CEO of Cadillac Fairview, said, "I just like to make good shoes. That's about it. If you are going to make shoes, make good shoes."

Asked why he enthusiastically took on the presidency of Steinberg Inc. after enjoying a very successful career as an entrepreneur, Irving Ludmer said, "Why do you do these things? Why do you climb Mount Everest? Because it's there, it's the challenge."

Then there is that often-mentioned characteristic, plain old *common sense*, the art of being realistic and an absence of wishful thinking. Effective leaders are practical. Those who succeed practice the art of the possible and are willing to tie their objectives to those of the organization.

Finally, there is the ability to *delegate with confidence*. Individuals at any level of responsibility in any position of power, regardless of the type of organization, can possess all the previously mentioned characteristics, but they are next to useless without the confidence to delegate authority to others in the organization. Alan Taylor, chairman and CEO of the Royal Bank of Canada, remarked:

> The best CEO must be a leader and he must display those leadership qualities all the time to the people who work directly with him. I don't think a CEO can do anything on his own for a long time. Implementation requires team effort and people believing, "Yes, I've got to do it".

Jean de Grandpré of Bell Canada Enterprises added his comments to the issue of delegation:

> I very seldom interfere with the decisions of what I call the service units or the profit centers or whatever you want to call them, as long as I have confidence in their judgment and in their capabilities. Sure, I'm going to follow their results and I'm going to interfere or intervene if there is a deterioration in whatever they do, but if I want people to be accountable, then I cannot substitute my judgment for theirs because they will say, "Sure my results are not that

good, you remember you said to do it this way and I followed your advice. I'm not telling you that your decision was wrong, but I'm telling you that it wasn't my decision." So all along, I have always managed with hands off. [I say,] "You are responsible for this type of operation, you run it. If you don't run it well, then I'm going to put in someone else to run it."

As we have stated, leadership is a rather remarkable mix of qualities, traits, values and skills. Specifically, leadership is a sense of direction, a clear ability to communicate and the enthusiasm and energy to motivate others in the organization. However, leadership appears to include one more key element—the inherent enjoyment of being in the top job. In summary, rather than being driven by insatiable appetites for power and position, successful CEOs simply love to lead.

CHAPTER

6

DIFFERING
SKILLS

L eadership incorporates certain skills. In this chapter we discuss the skills possessed by those who reach the top job in corporations, and how these skills evolve during a business career. Much of this material is based on appraisal results collected over five years from more than three thousand individuals, most of them men, in a variety of roles and levels within a wide range of industries. This mass of information permitted us to develop a profile of the "typical" first-level supervisor, middle manager and senior executive. It has permitted a number of statistical analyses of the data to determine the differences between people at various levels of management. In addition, our experience in working with hundreds of organizations has given us a sense of the evolution of these skills during an executive's career.

Let's look at some leadership skills and qualities.

Intelligence
What is important in management is the ability to solve problems. It takes intelligence to do this, so for the sake of simplicity we will use these terms interchangeably.

People in higher management levels score higher than the average on tests of problem-solving ability. The scores increase as the management level rises, and the range of scores narrows at successively higher levels. At entry-level positions, there is a very wide range of intellectual ability (as there is for nearly all the eighty-seven measures from our data base of appraisal results). The range of scores becomes narrower in middle-management positions because those with the lowest scores tend not to make it to managerial ranks. The dropping of individuals with lower scores continues at each successive managerial level; those who reach the top tend to be those with the higher scores. There is less variation because they all tend to come from the upper part of the distribution curve.

Executives seem to be ambivalent about intelligence. Most describe themselves modestly in this regard, yet one of their highest accolades for those they respect is that they are "very intelligent." Clearly, however, intelligence alone is not sufficient.

Gordon Farquhar of Aetna Canada placed common sense above intelligence in importance:

> I think it takes more common sense than sheer intelligence to function successfully as a CEO. What it really requires is practical intelligence, a sense of judgment, to be able to wade through the complexities and the chaff to find the key issue. One of the hardest things about the job is to reduce something to a manageable issue in order to find the solution.

William Richards, former president of Dome Petroleum Ltd., agreed:

> Intelligence is not paramount. I think you want a person with a little imagination. Often people who are too damn smart hesitate and worry and become incapacitated. They think of all the horrible possible outcomes and never get anything done. Then again, occasionally you encounter the highly intelligent person who lacks practical sense, and this person can become really dangerous.

A high score on an intelligence test does not automatically translate into success in management, but lack of intelligence almost always guarantees failure. Intelligence is an attribute that is essential but is not by itself sufficient for success as an executive.

Robert Hurlbut of General Foods explained:

> You don't have to be a great intellect, except in some jobs like strategic planning. The intellectual, I think, cannot identify with people and their needs and hence the markets. But you do have to be reasonably bright.

Richard Thomson of the Toronto-Dominion Bank holds an MBA from Harvard. He told us:

> We'd all like to think we are intelligent once we have made it. I think intelligence does help. It's interesting, that what you learn in school is not really what you need to know to run a business, but if you've got the ability to learn fast, that does show up in school. It gives you great confidence if you are good at learning. An executive needs that kind of confidence. You have got to keep educating yourself.

When looking at "problem-solving skills," we examined six separate abilities and assessed the skills of management in these areas.

The Ability To Reason In Abstract Terms

This type of thinking involves conceptualization and is important in work such as computer programming, advanced mathematics, the sciences and packaged-goods marketing. It is the only problem-solving measure on which the management population did not do much better than do high-school graduates. However, as one moves up the management ranks there is a gradual increase in score, and fewer of the top managers get low scores. Apparently this type of problem solving is not important to success in general management.

The Ability To Do Arithmetic

In spite of the widespread use of calculators and computers, the ability of managers to do basic arithmetic has, if anything, increased in the past ten years. This ability increases as one moves up the executive ranks. There are few individuals with low scores at the top. This result is not surprising since so much information about company operations is expressed in numbers.

The Ability To Work With Words
Communication is fundamental to management, and all management groups score significantly above average on a measure of vocabulary and the ability to speak and write clearly. Observation suggests that managers with poor verbal skills are at a great disadvantage and tend not to impress other executives. They are seen as less intelligent or at least as less effective. The average scores increase with the management level, and the number with low scores drops off quickly. Verbal skills are clearly one of the essential tools of senior executives.

The Ability To Work With Detail
One might not think the ability to work with detail is important for an executive, but executives far outshine high-school graduates in this. Most executives express a dislike for detail work, but most of them have to devote a good deal of their time to working with it.

The Ability To Solve Complex Problems
This type of thinking is required for logical analysis, evaluating arguments and drawing conclusions from a set of facts. All management levels do better than the general population, and the average performance increases as individuals advance in rank. Our observation suggests that executives who have come up through engineering, accounting, data processing or any line of work that places a high premium upon accuracy are likely to be slower and more cautious in solving problems. Such individuals prefer to have facts backed by data before they make a decision, and gathering the facts can be a time-consuming activity. Those with backgrounds in sales, marketing and general management are likely to solve problems faster because they tend to rely more on instinct. The best of all possible worlds is to be

fast and right; slow and right is next best, and other permutations are not very acceptable.

Our experience with executives suggests that problem-solving skills can be learned. Many companies provide courses for their employees designed to improve their skill in problem-solving. Education alone, however, cannot be expected to enhance these skills.

D.N. Perkins at Harvard University conducted a recent study published in the *Journal of Education Psychology*, which suggests that higher levels of education do not dramatically improve an individual's everyday reasoning skills. Perkins concluded, "Most educational practice does little to prepare students for reasoning out open-ended issues." He suggests that graduate schools, in particular, aim to create experts whose mental gymnastics will be exercised only in their field of study, and that improvement of their reasoning skills for life does not necessarily follow. Thus, college attainment alone is not a good measure of the ability of an individual to be successful in life or in business. Donald McCarthy, CEO of Beatrice Foods, made the point: "I've run into some real dummies who have done extremely well at university. That's not intelligence. I have seen some awfully sad cases where people got very good marks, but when you get them into decision-making roles and putting the facts together, they wonder what's going on."

Siegfried Streufert, at Pennsylvania State College of Medicine, in his book *Complexity, Managers and Organizations*, says that the best managers "are always strategizing. It's an overall approach. Most business schools don't teach this—they teach you what to think, not how to think." Not all business-school graduates agree. Larry Heisey, chairman and former CEO of Harlequin Enterprises Limited, went to Harvard.

> It was the first time in my life I was acutely aware that I was able to think. I had studied logic and knew what a syllogism was, but I was not aware that I could take disparate information and recompose it and come to conclusions. That was exciting!

The Ability To Learn Quickly

Some measures of problem-solving relate closely to the ability to deal quickly and effectively with written material. With the rapid changes in business and the amount of written information that must be assimilated, the ability to comprehend written material is an important skill. We have found what appears to be an upward shift in this ability in people in the top jobs over the last ten years.

Other Attributes

Understanding People

Many of the CEOs we interviewed stressed the importance of being able to get along with people—interpersonal skills. It is, of course, important for a CEO to make or endorse sound strategic decisions for the business, but if he lacks the ability to work effectively with subordinates, to make them feel part of the team and to gain their commitment to the goals of the enterprise, his chances of success are greatly reduced.

The level of interpersonal skills has increased at the top levels of management over the past ten years because CEOs have had to deal with increasingly sophisticated groups of individuals, including trade unions, shareholders, consumers and environmentalists. All management levels are stronger than the general population in this skill, and middle managers and executives are the strongest. Executives tend to be more realistic in the assessment of the motivation of others than those in the lower levels. They also tend to take themselves less seriously.

Tact, one component of social facility in the business environment, increases slightly as one moves up the management ladder. On average, senior executives—general managers, vice presidents and CEOs—show greater tact than do 70 percent of other people.

Practical Judgment

Managers at all levels have a higher level of practical judgment or the ability to solve concrete and immediate problems (as opposed to strategic problems) than the general population. Mid-level and top managers have similar levels, which are stronger than those of lower levels of management.

Edward Crawford, CEO of Canada Life Assurance Company, summarized his strength:

> I certainly have no great mathematical skill. I think I had one thing that was useful and still is the key to any successful CEO, and that is common sense and a practical point of view. In my mind, people who are highly talented in a technical way often lack that sort of common sense.

Approach to work

All levels of management place higher emphasis on the ability to think, plan and organize than the general population. As a group, managers were shown to be less motivated than the average person to do repetitive tasks. They would not perform well on an assembly line because they have a higher need for challenge and stimulation.

Interests

The emphasis placed on economic matters increases as one moves up the corporate ladder. Executives also show strong interest in power and prestige and in being involved in something of significance. Executives are no more concerned than the average person with theoretical considerations, but they are more pragmatic, being more concerned with what will work than they are with theory. They are less concerned than the average person with things of an aesthetic nature.

As one would expect, executives are interested in running things, in selling or negotiating and in communication. Technical interests are of low priority, as are the biological sciences, computation, social service, art and music.

Personality

Top managers are characterized by a dominant personality and a high energy level. In both these areas they are significantly higher than the general population. Individuals don't usually get to the top by happenstance. Instead they actively seek more challenge. A number of studies also show that managers are able to carry a demanding work load over a long period of time.

Managers are also more emotionally stable and can see themselves and their lives more objectively. In addition, they place more emphasis on getting things done without upsetting people, but will confront problems when necessary.

Managers are distinguished by a very high need for achievement, high optimism and self-confidence and a high level of self-sufficiency. As a group, managers do not need much support from their superiors. They are ready to take responsibility for their actions. They tend to prefer situations in which they have a modest amount of independence to decide how to achieve their objectives. As a group they do not have a high need for autonomy; rather they seem willing and able to fit in.

Executives like themselves and feel in control of their personal and professional lives. Most possess good social poise and are comfortable dealing with others.

Executives emphasize approaching their jobs in an organized and orderly way. While they are conventional and will draw upon past experience, they also believe in innovation and creativity, and will try to improve on the solutions to problems.

Knowledge and Experience
In the first half of the century, it was believed that an executive had to have experience in a business in order to run it. When the conglomerates came along, it was conventional wisdom that a manager could manage just about anything because the techniques were universal. Today knowledge of the industry and the specific company are again regarded as a major asset for those hoping to become CEO. More long-time employees are being appointed to the position of CEO; the proportion of high-level movers has decreased. Robert Gratton, CEO of Montreal Trust, observed:

I don't think that people can go from one CEO job to another in different industries easily and successfully. To run a company properly you have to understand the business very well. Otherwise you might make a decision without understanding its implications. I would never have had the confidence to propose my business plan if I had not been in the industry since I left school.

As recruiters, we have often observed that employers are not very interested in candidates with experience in an unrelated industry. If the individual's experience has been in an industry that is considered to be in decline, that, too, is a distinct handicap. The industry in which the applicant has experience colors and in some cases tarnishes the individual's appeal. One way to succeed is to choose an industry that is healthy and growing and will still be around when you are ready for the top job.

Some people, however, do move successfully into the top job from another field. Purdy Crawford, now CEO of Imasco, was formerly a senior partner in a law firm. Of his experience he said:

The skills that I bring I think got me to the right place at the right time. I feel I had a good sense from my previous background—that doesn't mean every lawyer has—of dealing with public policy issues, with shareholders and public relations, things that have been and will be a very important part of this company. On drug issues or tobacco, I'm not the leader, I'm the manager of the leader. But in public policy and financial matters I'm quite directly involved with cabinet ministers and with public servants, and that's an area I've visited before. I think I can communicate and deal with those people a lot better than a lot of CEOs or senior lawyers I've dealt with in the past. I've worked on public policy issues from a government perspective. I think the same is true in mergers and acquisitions. I visited that before in an advisory and hard-working service capacity. I make decisions easily and very quickly. I have no problem making decisions; if I've made the wrong one, life goes on.

Many aspects of management, such as interpersonal skills and attitudes, financial expertise and analytical techniques are transferable. But every business has its own unique challenges, which call for special knowledge. Jack Fraser, CEO of Federal Industries, takes the middle road.

> We will not put a president in a subsidiary who does not know the business. If you have a large company with good operational management, then bringing in an outstanding conceptual or strategic thinker could well play an extremely important part in re-directing the company. But that would work only if there was the strength of knowledge in and understanding of the company. You cannot be a great strategic thinker unless you have a pretty damn good knowledge of the industry you are in.

Evolving Executive Skills

To advance in business an individual must acquire new skills to meet new challenges, and must develop new attitudes toward his work and toward himself. The attitudes and skills that served in youth will not work when one is older and at a more senior level of management. What is appropriate at fifteen is not appropriate at thirty. What is appropriate for a clerk is not appropriate for a supervisor. In short, on the road to the top, one must learn to adapt.

All too often we see what happens when an employee fails to adapt. How many times has a company promoted their best salesperson to a management position only to find they have gained a poor manager and have lost a good salesperson? The skills and attitudes that make a successful salesperson are not the same as those required to manage. To succeed in sales, a person must be energetic, have good interpersonal skills, particularly on a one-on-one basis, and be able to withstand the frustration of being turned down. Salespeople find an immediate reward in getting an order, and they tend to be hands-on people who like to be where the action is. A sales manager, on the other hand, must be good at planning, organizing, supervising and training. The measure of success in sales management is not usually immediate and builds over time and that success when it comes is more subtly defined. The skills required of a sales manager are also different in nature. Managers are more intellectual and more oriented to solving problems. Some individuals are successful in both roles, either because they had both sets of skills or quickly developed the second, but not all salespeople have a manager hidden inside them.

We have identified six steps, each with its own skills, that an individual can pass through from the initial job-entry positions to the position of CEO. These "steps" do not necessarily parallel the levels of management in a corporation, but they do show a progression of development that most senior executives have passed through. Some individuals are unable or unwilling to make these transitions and consequently limit their advancement:

1. The sole contributor
2. The working supervisor
3. The department manager
4. The multidepartment manager
5. The strategic planner
6. The corporate manager

The Sole Contributor

The first job most people have is as a sole contributor, and many never move from this role. Sole contributors exist at numerous levels in organizations, from the lowest entry job to the senior branches. The distinguishing characteristics of this sort of job are that little or no supervision of others is involved and that one's contribution is based on one's own knowledge, skill and effort. One's effectiveness is not multiplied as it is when one coordinates or motivates others. It is the function of sole contributors either to carry out assigned tasks (usually with opportunity to help decide how it will be done but with little or no involvement in the overall direction or strategy), or to provide management with advice and guidance or services in their area of specialty.

While most of the jobs that fall into this category are clerical, the category also includes professional or

specialist positions, such as engineers, lawyers and doc-
tors. Some sole contributors can rise to a high level in an
organization, be well paid and recognized, while still per-
forming a specialist's role. For a number of people, the sole
contributor role is seen as a steppingstone to wider
responsibility and to management. But others view it as an
end in itself.

It is not so much intelligence that distinguishes between
groups at the senior level, but interest and self-perception.
Different people seek different kinds of satisfaction. For
some, money and power or prestige are strong motivators.
For others, however, the satisfaction derives from the work
itself, from meeting a challenge, from solving a problem.
These individuals often gravitate to the sole contributor role.

It often happens that success as a sole contributor is
taken as an indication of an individual's potential for
promotion. Sometimes the indication is not correct or fair.
It is at this career point that a major change or discontinuity is found in the skill set required for success. For
example, the characteristics that make a good engineer or
other specialist relate to their specific body of knowledge
and their personal work attitudes. But what happens when
such a person is promoted to a supervisory role? The job
and its demands on the individual change considerably.
This person must now concern himself with the selection,
training and supervision of subordinates; he must organize, plan and communicate. He must make some contribution to the overall planning of the function, and possibly interact with other supervisors. For some people
these changes come as a welcome challenge, and the indication that they are now on their way to bigger and better things; others experience a sense of loss. They miss the
direct use of their technical expertise. They miss the freedom of movement; they feel they are moving paper and
are no longer where the action is. These feelings mark the
difference between the sole contributor and the manager.

The Working Supervisor
The first step up from a sole contributor is supervision of
others doing what one formerly did oneself. Often this

move brings with it the expectation that one will continue to do some of the previous job oneself. In the factory, the lead hand is representative of this level, as is the sales manager who retains his own territory. This step represents something of a "halfway house," which preserves contact with the familiar and comfortable, while introducing new and challenging skills.

It is in this role that one begins to feel like a manager and to understand the difference between achieving through one's own efforts and achieving through others. This role brings with it the first indications of the "costs" involved in moving to management. These costs include: the loss of direct contact with "the action," the frustration of trying to get others to do things when you know you could do them better yourself, the longer time frame required to measure success, the less obvious relationship between your effort and success, the need to develop greater tolerance for ambiguity and the feeling that your job is never done.

For some people, this sort of role is an ideal compromise, because it involves a bit of both worlds. Some of these jobs exist in the upper echelons of a corporation and provide great challenge, involvement and visibility. A good example of this role is the vice president and corporate counsel of a large corporation who is part of the senior management group. In this position, the individual brings professional expertise to a wide range of business problems, from the mundane to those that profoundly influence the success and survival of the corporation.

The Department Manager

The working supervisor, like the sole contributor, often finds a place in a variety of levels in an organization. It can be a step on the way to management, or it can be an extension of the sole contributor role. Department management, on the other hand, is often an unequivocal move to management. This role brings with it much less "doing" than the individual has experienced before, and much more planning, training, supervising, appraising and management. It requires the person to learn and exercise skills in supervision and motivation, and it brings with it a new sort of management challenge: coordinating and interacting with peers in different functions. This interaction requires the development of a wider understanding of company operations as well as a deep understanding of the specific function for which the person is responsible. In this role, a person must begin to be a generalist and to develop the ability to put his or her specialty into the perspective of the total company operation. To do this, the person must also learn to compromise between conflicting pressures.

At this point the person must begin to see himself or herself in a different light—no longer the engineer, the accountant, the specialist of some sort, but a manager—manager knowledgeable in specific areas, but whose major skills now should be of a more general nature.

The Multi Department Manager

This is the middle-management level of responsibility, the manager of managers. The skill discontinuity in this position is more a matter of degree than it is of kind since the multi department manager requires more of the same skills as the department manager. At this level, the manager is even more removed from "the action," and exerts control by interacting with other managers. There is room for differing styles of management, but what the multi manager accomplishes is done by influencing other managers. The position can involve much more counseling and advising. The time span over which results are obtained is greater, and long-range planning begins to take precedence over immediate or everyday activities. Once again, the time it takes to find out if one has done a good job increases, so that there is less immediate feedback than at lower levels.

Some new skills may be required at this stage, but the major changes are in attitude. Being a multi department manager requires a broader outlook, and the ability to work with less certainty and to cope with the feeling that the job is never done.

The Strategic Planner

This step is not necessarily a sequential one, as the earlier ones have been. Rather, it marks the point at which the focus of the job moves from primarily in-company orientation or specialization to involvement with the total business. At this point the person involved becomes a general manager (with or without that title) and is required to understand the functioning of the company as an entity within the wider context of its industry and the economy. There are specialists in strategic planning, but these individuals serve as staff to the individual we are considering now. It is these general management people who must make the decisions that determine the direction of the company. They have by this time lost their identification with the specialty with which they entered the business world and are now managers in the widest sense of the word.

The skills and attitudes required to make this step are not fundamentally different from those at previous levels, but there must be an ability to cope with pressure, ambiguity and uncertainty. Generally, managers at this stage need strong intellectual skills, specifically the ability to think through complex problems and to reach solutions that will work effectively. Physical and mental stamina, always important, are increasingly critical in this position. The focus of the job is primarily the future, and involvement with day-to-day "action" is reduced to a fraction.

The Corporate Manager

At this point almost all the day-to-day management activities are delegated to others and the corporate manager must exercise new skills and attitudes. These relate to the ability to delegate much more to others, to give more general direction, to develop involvement, to take a longer-term view and to attend to the outside public. The CEO's function as a figurehead is important because he symbolizes the company to employees as well as to government, the media, the client base and the general public. In many ways, he becomes the embodiment of the corporation's personality and what it stands for.

Bernard Ghert, in speaking of the changes necessary at this juncture in his career, said:

I think people would say I have changed. The biggest change was in trying to understand the motivation of others. I've become a bit of a cynic, maybe less trusting— less direct. I used to just tell people what was right, what we do. But that didn't work. You have to decide that you're going to get what you want. People are going to do it because they want to do it. It is a matter of motivating them both internally and externally. This is the cynical part: people will only do things if they see it is in their interest. Whenever anyone deals with you it is basically in his interest. You have to analyze very carefully and think about what is in it for him. What's his motivation? Why is he going to do it? And if he does something you ask him to do, what are you going to owe him in the future?

Skills

The career steps we have outlined are simplifications. Actually, they can occur in different ways in a person's career. But in general, these six steps move a person through first-level supervision to mid-level manager and on to senior executive positions. We have identified ten strongly developed characteristics common to each of the three levels:

- speed of learning
- verbal skills
- complex problem-solving
- speed and accuracy in detail
- interpersonal skills
- knowledge of supervisory techniques
- knowledge of sales techniques
- interest in selling
- practical judgment
- dominance

More important, we have concluded that there are significant differences in the levels of each of these skills between first-level supervisors and mid-level managers, and again between mid-level managers and executives. The differences are sufficiently wide that it is possible, using test scores alone, to separate first-level supervisors from mid-level managers 69 percent of the time, and mid-level managers from executives with 80 percent accuracy.

Knowing one's own skills and attitudes can often help one find the right position. Steven Wilgar, CEO of Warner-Lambert in Canada, found this out years ago when he left his position as CEO of the Canadian company to assume a corporate role at the American head office. He took over responsibility for supervising the corporation's subsidiaries in Latin America, a job that gave him a very small corporate staff and a great deal of travel. After a couple of years he was given responsibility for the Pacific Rim subsidiaries, but travel and communications problems were, if anything, more demanding.

> You come across something and you want to talk to somebody, you look at your watch and it's four in the afternoon. It's four in the bloody morning in Japan! It might be two in the morning or six o'clock, but you still say, "How the hell am I going to get to him?" You just couldn't get your arms around it to get the same kind of satisfaction. It simply was not satisfying.

Wilgar found that he derived his satisfaction from feeling part of something, from participating and from influencing others. But as head of Pacific Rim subsidiaries, he felt a lack of influence. (The only major decision he could likely make was to go with or to replace the local president.) This feeling, together with the travel and the consequent cost to his family life, resulted in dissatisfaction. He was determined to move. The opportunity to return to the presidency of the Canadian company arose and he took it.

Wilgar's story is unusual. Retracing steps is rarely possible. The decision to make such a move required Wilgar to sort out his priorities carefully and to consider what he did well and what he enjoyed doing. This led him to accept the reappointment, because it provided the best combination of elements: an industry he knew, a good-sized company to run, status within the community, the country of his roots and the ability to maintain the family life-style he wanted. The cost was the risk of seeming to take a backward step or of having failed. Concern for what others will think is a very human characteristic, and one that takes determination to overcome.

Many factors influence the ability and freedom of the individual to move through the stages of management growth. Some are obvious, such as lack of ability or training. Less obvious but nonetheless real are the factors of attitude, values and life-style. We often discover through trial and error just what we want and the price we are ready to pay for it. Often the price is not real to us until the bill comes, and then it may be too late to make a change.

The conventional wisdom in our society is that one should be ambitious and seek "more"; this is hard to resist because getting ahead has its rewards. Even if one has misgivings about accepting a promotion or transfer because it does not meet personal objectives, it is often hard to resist.

The unassuming Donald McCarthy, CEO of Beatrice Foods, had been with Nestlé Canada for some twenty-three years, the last few as president when the chairman of the Swiss parent company presented him with the opportunity to move to Switzerland for two years in international marketing, and then to move to the presidency of a subsidiary in some other part of the world. This move was not attractive to McCarthy, but he accepted it anyway. He soon realized, though, that even with a beautiful house with a fantastic view over Lake Geneva to the French Alps, he was not happy at the prospect of joining a select group of rootless international executives. When an opportunity arose to become president of William Neilson Limited in Toronto, McCarthy took the job. After several years, he was moved to the corporate office as group executive and given responsibility for a number of companies, including Neilson's. He enjoyed this for a few years, but soon the challenges became fewer, and he moved to Beatrice, where he had the degree of hands-on involvement he wanted and the challenge of a large and diversified operation. Donald McCarthy reflected:

> I knew it was right for me to make a change. I've always had the conviction that if you are really unhappy in either

your personal life or your business life, you change. Do
something about it, don't just live with it.

The job of the CEO requires a wide variety of skills. No list
can hope to be complete, and ours certainly is not. It does,
however, give some indication of the basic attributes of
problem-solving skills, skills with people and some personality characteristics that differentiate senior executives
from lower-level managers and the general population.

As we noted, one set of skills and attitudes is not sufficient to take someone from entry-level jobs to the top job.
The nature of the job changes as one moves up the ranks,
and the skills necessary to meet the new challenges change
as well. Possessing the attributes we have mentioned does
not guarantee success, but lacking them much reduces the
likelihood of reaching the top job. Above all, knowing
one's own skills, limits and motivations often allows an
executive to find the right place and level to find real satisfaction and to fulfill his ambition.

CHAPTER

7

THE PRICE
OF SUCCESS

W e have heard people at all levels of employment say
that they don't want promotions, usually because
they think that the rewards of the position are not sufficient to compensate for the costs. The costs are usually
seen as heavier responsibility, additional stress, long hours,
heavy travel schedules, less time for spouse and children
and less time to pursue other interests.

The leadership qualities shown by many of our chief executive officers go beyond the tremendous energy and
hours that they devote directly to their corporations. Most
of them must also contribute their efforts toward the outside world—the business community, the community at
large, associations, charities and the like. Often their involvement is not purely social; it includes a leadership role,
such as the presidency of a hospital foundation, the
chairmanship of a charitable organization or the management of some special social-action project.

Chief executive officers find various ways to justify the
endless hours such external activities take. Some point out
that although the corporation's main objectives are profits

and return on investment, it should also return something to society—responsible social behavior. Gerald Hobbs, formerly of Cominco, commented:

> My view is that a company that makes its living in a country or a region has an obligation to be a good citizen of that region, in the sense of supporting the things that are being undertaken in the region or country that are valuable to the society. It has to be a personal involvement, as well as a corporate one. I'm not talking about spending corporate money for personal aggrandizement, but putting your money where you put your effort.

Michael Cornelissen, the young and aggressive CEO of Royal Trust, is a strong advocate of chief executive officers having an active role in the community. He told us:

> Business executives have four important constituents competing for their time and attention: one is his or her job, the second is the family, the third is physical and mental well-being and the fourth is community activities. It is important to find the right balance among the four, each of which have different priorities, but are nevertheless important for different reasons.

Cornelissen's call for balance is often hard to achieve. All too often, CEOs talked about the endless number of external engagements and outside activities they are asked to attend. It is hard for them to say no. Charles Hantho of C-I-L reflected on this dilemma and what he has learned:

> First of all, it's a bottomless pit out there of things you could get involved in, and you really must have discipline right from the beginning. If I had to do it over I'm sure there are some things I would have accepted and other things I wouldn't have accepted. It's flattering to be asked to get involved in all these things, and if you're not careful, you'll actually believe they're asking you as an individual as opposed to the office you hold.

Some CEOs have little trouble in saying no. They believe that the corporation's job is to enhance the shareholders' value, and that isn't accomplished by social activity. They apply this belief not only to themselves, but also to their employees. Community activities cost the company a great deal in dollars and time and distract employees from their jobs. Moreover, they point out that choosing among the often differing objectives of volunteer organizations can be troublesome.

Most CEOs, however, agree with Trevor Eyton. He explained:

> There are two reasons you do good for the community. One is to help your community and the other is to help yourself. It's a part of the mosaic in Canada, and if you go to almost any important community function you tend to see the same two or three hundred faces that most people identify as the most successful people in the community.

There is a consensus among the majority of corporate leaders that efforts devoted to the outside world can be good for employee morale, good for the corporation's image, good for developing stronger links between employees and communities and, of course, good for the organizations that receive their support. Because they are leaders, CEOs set the example, even at a cost to themselves. To a number of CEOs it is an important obligation. Robert Martin, of Consumers' Gas, said:

> You've got to put something back. I believe that about my own life. I have difficulty saying no to anyone who asks me to do something for a good cause yet it burns up a lot of my time. It is the community that supports my business. I have a social responsibility to be part of that community.

Leadership, be it within the corporation or without, is a time-consuming responsibility. It takes dedication and self-discipline.

Yet the majority of CEOs we spoke with discussed the job in terms of "fun" or "challenge," and most would not willingly give it up. It is rare to find people who have stepped back from the job because they have decided that their personal cost-benefit analysis came out on the negative side.

Some of the benefits of the job are apparent to even the most casual readers of the business pages. The financial rewards can be excellent and in some cases mind-boggling. In addition, there are the executive toys—the jets, limousines and club memberships—in short, the opportunity to live very well. The job brings status and the ability to influence events.

However, almost every CEO we spoke with had some comment on the cost of the job and many spoke of the need for an understanding, strong and supportive wife to fill in the gaps the CEO's schedule left in the family life. Edward Crawford, CEO of Canada Life, told us:

> One's spouse is key. It is the essential factor in the whole thing because the person is part of the team. We have meetings and conferences where you are expected to bring your spouse with you. She plays a role in trying to build a team spirit, and goes out of her way to meet the wives of others and also the other people in the business.

With or without a supportive spouse, CEOs find that their jobs can cause family problems. Many expressed regret at the lack of time they had to be with their children. Peter Gordon, retired CEO of Stelco, felt that there was a cost to family life as he moved up the executive ranks.

> I think my family life has suffered. My children were really raised by my wife because I was working eighteen hours a day, and when I wasn't working I spent time with other people in the organization. I was devoted to this place seven days a week.

Melvin Hawkrigg was luckier. He was able to be home more during his children's formative years. He said:

> Now I'm at home for dinner one night a week, whereas before I was at home most of the time. Earlier in my career, when the children were young, I worked close to home, so I could work twelve-hour days and still have dinner with the little guys. I spent a lot of time with them because I love sports and all of the kids played hockey and baseball and I was usually there. I would move heaven and earth to get to the kids' games.

Robert Hurlbut, retired CEO of General Foods, told us:

> In the early days when I was a product manager I worked
> long hours and the weekends. My wife was young and
> prepared to roll with it and we didn't have children for a
> few years and so I wasn't neglecting the parental respon-
> sibility. If it is necessary or desirable for you to spend most
> of your time through the week as well as weekends with
> your family, I guess I failed. It would have been nice to
> have been available to take the boys to a ball game more of-
> ten, but I don't think they were terribly shortchanged. I
> would do the same thing all over again.

Louis Hollander, CEO of Canada Colors and Chemicals,
agreed:

> I literally worked seven days a week. As my wife says, I
> have gone from working fifteen-hour days to working ten-
> hour days, seven days a week. I did that for five days a
> week and some of Saturday and Sunday from about 1970 to
> 1985. There was a price to pay, but it was a conscious deci-
> sion. I wasn't forced into it, I said I wanted to do it. The
> time I did have available on the weekends I spent with the
> children, the family. I don't think they have paid a price
> and they don't either.

Robert Martin, CEO of Consumers' Gas, recollected the
early job pressures.

> I've indirectly paid a price. In the early years when I was
> under a lot of pressure, I had to work long hours and on
> weekends because I was a young guy with a big respon-
> siblity that I took very seriously. My wife wasn't very
> happy with the amount of time I was away from home. I
> had no other interests than my job. She had to really beat
> on me to take holidays. I don't think I had enough time to
> smell the roses. I paid a price in that some of the things I'd
> like to have done, some of the social contacts I would have
> liked to develop, I just didn't and still don't have time for.

Most CEOs recognize the heavy load their jobs placed on
their spouses. Their wives often ran the home and a
family single-handed. Sometimes this pressure and the

differing interests and lives of the partners caused
problems in the marriages. In other instances the business and social demands brought about a closeness that
enhanced the marriage. Robert Kadlec, CEO of Inland
Natural Gas, said:

> For my wife and me it has been a ball! I think that if there
> has been a price it has been our son and daughter. Until
> they were about eighteen we were able to spend a lot of
> time with them, but for the last few years, I simply have
> not had the time, and that I do regret. But my wife and I
> have had more time to be together and talk, and we can af-
> ford to do things now that we couldn't do before. I have
> her join me in a lot of things I do.

A few CEOs simply refuse to subordinate all else to the insatiable demands of the job. James Burns, CEO of Power
Financial Corporation is one of them. Burns, a graduate of
Harvard who spent much of his career in the insurance
business, moved from Winnipeg to Chicago, where he was
director of marketing for Great-West Life before becoming
president. He knew only too well that family life would
suffer if he allowed business to invade his personal life. He
said:

> In Montreal and Toronto, two business dinners a week are
> almost compulsory. I never accept an invitation to a busi-
> ness dinner. If somebody says "We'll meet and talk about it
> over dinner," I say, "No, I have dinner at home. If you want
> to see me, you see me during the day."

Charles Hantho of C-I-L talked about cutting back on outside obligations.

> You think you should accept a lot of invitations to
> represent a presence for C-I-L in the business community.
> But I have now become very ruthless about deciding
> which ones I accept, and I'm turning down four for
> every one I accept. I'm still out two or three nights a
> week and I work a twelve-hour day and without fail I'm
> in at eight o'clock in the morning and I never leave
> before six-thirty.

Richard Thomson, of the Toronto Dominion Bank, commented on different work habits:

> To me there are two kinds of executives. One kind goes to meetings all the time, has his calendar chock full and is proud of the fact that if you phone and say, "I'd like to have a meeting with you," he'd say, "Well, I can fit you in a week from now." I think I'm probably the exact opposite. I will try to fit you in any day. Obviously I can't always do it but I try to keep periods of every day free purposely because I like to read.

The need to move from city to city as one climbs the ladder also has its price. Donald McIvor, former CEO of Imperial Oil, said:

> We are now in our twelfth or thirteenth house, and we have had apartments, too. I think for most women, and I have talked to many women about this, it is not the preferred mode of existence. I believe my children are more sophisticated than children who lived out their early lives in just one spot. It is all trade-offs, and the question is, what did they pay for that?

Allan Taylor, CEO of the Royal Bank of Canada, another executive who has faced many moves in his career, remarked:

> Tremendous support from your wife is absolutely necessary. I think I would have a hard time identifying many CEOs from large corporations where there hasn't been some problem in the family. It's better for family life to be in one spot. There is a lot more stability. It has to do with the education of your children and their ability to absorb and take changes. I happen to think that our children were in many ways better for the moves they had, but not in the matter of education. During the seven or eight years I was in senior international positions, I wasn't around a lot and I think the children suffered as a result. The kids would have liked a more regular family life; they saw the other kids' fathers at home at five or six o'clock and the family going off to do something that night, but I was off at a cocktail party or a business dinner or I was in New York. Often their mother had to be with me as well.

Demands on time and family are expected but some negative aspects of the job came as a surprise to new CEOs.

One of these aspects is the fact that there are always problems. When Robert Morison of Consumers Packaging assumed the job of CEO, Bud Reiger, one of the directors of the company, said to him, "You know, you've got two or three divisions, and I know your ambition is to get everything running exactly right all the time. It won't happen. There will always be something crop up all the time." Morison recalled, "He was right. We are doing all right as a corporation today, but there is always some problem. You push one down over there, and another one pops up over here."

The problems are not always foreseeable. Reflecting over his stewardship of the Royal Bank, Rowland Frazee said:

> You know what happened in 1982. We went into tailspin, a massive recession, and then we had the failure on some loans in the energy area and so forth. To me, the biggest disappointment was that we had kept our eyes on the ball, we had great strength in the retail bank, and 1986 was going to be the turnaround year, and then in January the oil crisis hit us right between the eyes. Maybe we should have anticipated it, but I don't think many people thought it would be that bad. So that's a disappointment. I don't know what I could have done differently in that context, but it was a failure. I guess I wouldn't be human if I didn't realize there had been some failures.

Gordon Farquhar recalled the time he was CEO of Aetna:

> It's fun 90 percent of the time. When it's not fun is when surprises occur, like when the director of finance walks in saying there had been an error in the second-quarter tax calculations, and the earnings will be down. Now, I'm the one who has to explain that to the directors!

Another fact that surprises new CEOs is how little they know about what is going on in the company. David McCamus said:

> There was one thing that surprised the heck out of me when I became president. I knew everybody, and suddenly

the communication stopped. I told them that I was the same guy, but they said I wasn't: now I was the president and they couldn't talk to me. I agree with an article I read recently that said the toughest job of the CEO is finding out what's going on!

Somewhat related was the comment of Richard Thomson of the Toronto-Dominion Bank:

> You can never get all the information you need to make a good decision. If you wait until you get all the information it is too late. I think that is one of the reasons it is important to have the right people around you. Once you have the right people, it is the CEO's job to decide where you are going to go and how you are going to get there. I think those who are not CEOs think that if they ever got there they could ram things through and change this or that. Well, once you get there you find out how hard it is to change anything.

The CEO has to cope with considerable pressure and stress. As one said, "There are some periods in the year when stress builds up because there is not enough time to do everything that absolutely has to be done. But for 90 percent of the time the stress of making decisions doesn't worry me at all. I think I thrive on a certain amount of stress, but sometimes it gets too much.

Bob DeMone spoke of his time as CEO of Maple Leaf Mills:

> The job is much tougher than I ever thought it would be and is getting tougher all the time. After I became CEO I had a year of extraordinary time commitments, but I kept saying to everybody that it was just for a year and would pass. Then I became chairman, president and CEO and the job has taken on a tremendous time constraint for me. It involves ever-increasing time and effort.

The ability to live with the pressure and stress is characteristic of successful CEOs.

Trevor Eyton of Brascan confided:

> Obviously there are parts of the job that are less pleasant
> than others, including the media abuse you get from time
> to time. Some of it is misdirected and I guess some of it
> comes close to the mark, but your life tends to become an
> open book. A lot of demands are made of you, some of
> which you welcome and some of which you don't. That's a
> mix everybody has got.

For some, the fact that the measure of their accomplish-
ments is often far in the future is dissatisfying. Bernard
Ghert of Cadillac Fairview said:

> It is harder to get satisfaction as time goes on because the
> things you do have a longer term and less measurable im-
> pact. When, as vice president of finance, you win a Toronto-
> Dominion Centre assessment case, you know you've done
> that. When you get the Eaton Centre financed and you see
> it under construction, then you know you've got something
> done. Now, some of the battles are very long.

A similar feeling is expressed by those who have moved
from being CEO of one company to a holding company
where they are responsible for the performance of several
companies. Melvin Hawkrigg experienced a difficult tran-
sition:

> I would say that the adjustment was mind-boggling. You
> would see something in a company that you thought
> should be done and would want to get in there and do it.
> That was the role I had had. I survived the year and now I
> really don't have any desire to run a company anymore,
> but for a year and a half I would dearly have loved to go in
> and run the trust company or the life company. I don't have
> that any more.

The loneliness of the top job is legendary. It was expressed
well by Angela Cantwell Peters, retired CEO of Bowering
Brothers Limited before its sale.

> The thing is it's very lonely there. It's terrible. Especially
> when Bowerings was being sold, I found I had nobody I

could talk to, and I couldn't bring it home. In spite of that, I
loved the job. It is stimulating and challenging. It is nice to
be able to run something, to make your own assessments. I
was comfortable in the company, it was like home to me, so
I wanted it to work.

Rowland Frazee of the Royal Bank reflected:

I have never met a CEO who wasn't ambitious or one who
doesn't have ego. The ambitions of a CEO are never satisfied
by having gotten to the top, but only when the objectives of
the corporation are met.

The top job clearly makes many heavy demands on the in-
cumbents, both on the way to it and there. Most CEOs do
not count the cost as too high. Perhaps those who would,
have eliminated themselves or have been eliminated. The
cost is great, but so are the challenges and rewards, and
few would willingly give the job up. For whatever reasons,
achievement by corporate leaders is not as highly recognized as achievement by leaders in many other fields of
endeavor—the arts, public service, entertainment, sport
and even the professions. Probably the price that they pay
is in large part not understood either. Interestingly, few
CEO's complain about this lack of understanding. In large
part they are a pretty pragmatic group. David McCamus
summed it up:

One of the aspects of being a hired gun is you never really
win. You just get to play another day. Another way of
saying it is: you're only as good as your last quarter of your
last football game. But it's exciting.

RELATIONSHIPS

Much of the chief executive officer's time is devoted to maintaining relationships both within the organization he leads and in the markets served by that organization. Much of a CEO's success is measured by the strength and the effectiveness of these relationships. We have chosen to discuss three key relationships. Two of these are internal. The first deals with how the CEO builds and manages his executive team; the second focuses on his relationship with the body he is accountable to—the board of directors. The third relationship is one of many that are part of the corporation's complex external environment, the one we believe is the most difficult for the CEO to deal with—that with government.

8

THE
EXECUTIVE
TEAM

O nce in the position, most chief executive officers come to realize that they cannot do it all alone. It's not that they don't accept their responsibilities, it's that they admit their dependency on a strong executive team. There was a time when many organizational leaders were reluctant to delegate authority to those below them, or to include subordinates in key decision-making. Perhaps they thought they would be perceived as lacking power. Today, it is quite different: CEOs are far more comfortable with collective decision-making and teamwork than they once were. Larry Heisey, CEO of Harlequin Enterprises, described his technique for collective decision-making:

> In the early years we [he and the five members of his team] used to meet two nights a week starting at 4:30 to 5:00. We'd crack open the bar and talk about the business. We reviewed the next day to make sure we hadn't gotten way off-base. Everyone had their input and they thought they were pretty good ideas.

The late Val Stock who was CEO of Canada Packers, talked about sharing authority and decision-making.

> The real problem is how much you interfere and how much do you not interfere. I have always worked from a philosophy that you give people a fair amount of freedom. You set objectives and certain targets and then you monitor people fairly closely and you discuss the problems with them and expect them to discuss them with you. But you try to work it out so that they are essentially running their own business.

Gordon Farquhar, former CEO of Aetna Canada, told us that listening is the essence of the CEO's role. "The ability to listen, to absorb differing points of view, to try not to legislate, but identify a course of action that is a good option, a good balance of conflicting views is an important aspect of the CEO's role."

In many corporations the leader's role is split and many of the CEO's duties are delegated to a key number-two man, who is usually called the *chief operating officer*. Once the chief executive officer and the chief operating officer were nicknamed "Mr. Outside" and "Mr. Inside," as a way of differentiating their roles. The growing importance of Mr. Outside paralleled the increasing complexity of the external environment and the marketplace. Mr. Outside saw to it that the affairs of state did not lose direction. Mr. Inside was supposed to keep his head down and concentrate on the day-to-day details of the internal operations. But it was never that simple. The chief executive officer, no matter how much he may have needed or wanted to focus on the outside, was accountable for *all* aspects of the organization. He could not and should not be isolated from the internal decision-making of the company. As Harold Geneen, in his book *Managing*, so bluntly puts it: "Management must manage."

Of course, there are always exceptions. Robert Bandeen reflects back on his years at CN when Donald Gordon was the CEO.

> Donald Gordon, in his last three years as chairman, never did really run CN. He wasn't a hands-on manager. He was a

banker. He didn't have experience operating a railroad. He did not run anything in that company. He was a public animal, but he gave leadership, and every person out there felt a part of something important because of Donald Gordon.

Of late, the numbers of top executives working closely with the CEO have risen. Now it is not unusual to have four or five key confidants working as an integrated management team together with the chief executive officer. Thus, in the lexicon of the corporate business world, there is a growing trend toward the use of the term "executive office" to refer to the two or more top executives who collectively share and carry out many of the CEO's responsibilities, duties and activities, except those that cannot be shared: the ultimate accountability for performance and the choice of what responsibilities will, in fact, be shared within the executive office.

Formal written definitions of the shared duties of the executive office rarely exist. Such job descriptions do not work at this level. Obviously, good working relationships must be developed and maintained, but they come about largely through personal arrangements. Most important, these arrangements work only when there is complete confidence and trust between the chief executive officer and his subordinate or subordinates. Communication must be easy and goals mutually understood. Above all, the whole arrangement has to be kept simple.

A number of years ago, we helped to introduce the concept of an executive office to a major Canadian company by suggesting that, rather than trying to differentiate the duties of the two top executives on the traditional outside-inside theme, the two work informally within the context of a general understanding. Broadly, the concept was that key strategic planning, public affairs and major financial decisions would rest with the chief executive officer, while other matters would be generally directed by the chief operating officer.

Initially, this concept did not work well. In fact, it caused problems between the two individuals and confusion in the ranks. Decisions were simply not being made. The chief operating officer was convinced he had all the problems without the authority to act, while the chief executive officer became increasingly frustrated because he could see little good happening even though he was bending over backward to give his COO room to maneuver.

Attempts at redefining roles failed to rectify matters. A third member was then introduced to the executive office. He was an executive vice president who was skilled at dealing with people and communications. It was hoped that these skills would bring some harmony to the situation. But instead, the chief operating officer became more insulated (and isolated), the chief executive officer more anxious and the executive vice president more confused. A far cry from the original intention!

Ultimately, the chief operating officer was replaced by the executive vice president, and the situation changed. The executive office has worked most successfully and has indeed been further expanded. The difference: a matter of compatible personalities, of mutual trust and of mutual confidence. The absence of those factors at the beginning doomed the first attempt to failure.

When you ask chief executive officers what skills they seek in key associates when forming their executive office, most talk about attitude. They usually want people they are comfortable with, people whose personalities are compatible not only with their own, but also with those of others on the team. And people who are good leaders, who are competitive and who are capable of looking ahead and talking intelligently about the future. Ultimately, and most important, they choose people whose opinions they respect. Bob DeMone, at the time CEO of Maple Leaf Mills and now CEO of Canadian Pacific Hotels, put it this way:

> I guess I look for people like myself. People who are able to take responsibility for their own actions, who have minds of their own, who are following a plan that has a beginning and an end and who are accountable for their results. I guess it's not untypical to look for people who are similar to yourself and that's not necessarily good.

Rolland Frazee, former CEO of the Royal Bank, added:

> I think an organization, to some extent, takes on the personality of the chief executive. The thing most likely to contribute to these [successful] changes is the organization that you establish underneath you and the people you put in those jobs. And that's why, over a period of time, you are not going to put people in jobs who have bad chemistry with you.

When asked what he looks for in divisional presidents, Louis Hollander, CEO of Canada Colors and Chemicals, replied:

> A nose for the dollar. A sense of how to make a profit. And a strong sense of values. I mean that in the context of courage, ethics, integrity and support for their people. I can cope and work much better with a man who is not a genius, but who has a strong sense of what needs to be done and gets on with it, and who works openly with me.

Lorne Lodge, the former CEO of IBM, put it in plain language:

> No one player makes the team. You've got to get good team players. No matter what job I had, I tried very early in the game to strengthen the people I had working with me.

Often those in the executive office with the chief executive officer wear two hats. The first hat represents the executive's primary operational responsibility to a particular component part (division or function) or parts of the organization. This responsibility is more or less clearly defined. The second hat represents the executive's role as the trusted extension of the CEO. The first hat is normally delegated on the basis of the executive's background and skills. The second hat is usually delegated on the basis of the CEO's evaluation of the individual's strengths. The greater the trust and confidence, the more sharing there is when dealing with strategic issues.

The chief executive officers with whom we talked clearly saw themselves as having to take full responsibility for 1) overall performance and growth of the enterprise, 2) the future direction and the sustained commitment to ongoing renewal and improvement and 3) the spirit of the enterprise—the clear retention and enhancement of the organization's values. This last responsibility is critical but sometimes forgotten. Values exist in every organization. They set the tone, and this tone is seen in those who work in the organization and in those whose lives it affects.

Many leaders today seek to share their responsibilities with their top team in the executive office. Even the difficult task of maintaining good relationships with one's board of directors is increasingly being shared, as other members of the executive office participate in the reporting duties at board meetings. The extent to which a CEO shares such activities depends on how much confidence he has in his team members, the degree to which they have an effect on the company and the time he and they have available to deal with the matter at hand.

Michel Bélanger, the CEO of The National Bank of Canada, reinforced the point.

> I seldom make a decision entirely on my own. When a tough decision is required, when I am concerned about something or it comes from one part of the organization or from outside, then I will at least consult the chief operating officer and possibly one of the others.

Recent surveys, such as the Conference Board of Canada research report "Chief Executives view their jobs: today and tomorrow," point to the fact that participative decision-making at the top is being given far more prominence today than in the past. The report points out: "Humility is not a characteristic often associated with CEOs. But they concede it when confronted with the implications that flow from large, corporate-wide decisions."

In response to the Conference Board survey, close to three hundred international CEOs reported on their approach to making major decisions. Ninety percent either said they did not make decisions alone or said they "tell [their] plans, listen to reactions, then decide." Twenty-five percent of these two groups admitted to a style aimed at developing a consensus while a further 30 percent agreed they preferred to listen to recommendations and then decide. Many did choose to say they used multiple approaches. The interesting trend, however, is toward the participation of others in the decision-making process. It confirms our conclusion that the increasing complexity of the top job is causing CEOs not only to actively seek the advice and counsel of key subordinates but also to have them share in the decision-making process. The more collegial style of the committee structure is definitely on the rise.

There are decisions, however, that the chief executive officer can never really share with his executive team, those that relate to his executive organization and to how he organizes and recognizes the key functions of his organization. It is up to him to ensure that the right people are in the right place at the right time to perform the right tasks. The CEO must decide alone on this one vital activity and he must rely on his own judgment. It is, in the end, his most important job because, done right, it ensures the development of a key, though small, cadre of leaders from which his successor will in all probablity be chosen.

This does not mean, however, that the CEO must write orderly and systematic definitions of jobs, policies and procedures. Fortunately, this rather bureaucratic approach to defining positions seems to be disappearing at the upper levels of many organizations. Rather, it is the task of the CEO to differentiate lines of business, to focus key management attention on strategic units and to create meaningful integrating mechanisms between them.

Many CEOs organize their operations around what are popularly referred to as strategic business units. Each of these units is composed of all those operating and staff functions directly related to a particular line of business. For example, Bell Canada Enterprises distinguishes between its regulated telephone operations of Bell Canada and its manufacturing arm, Northern Telecom, and its printing business, BCE PubliTech, and its real-estate development operations, BCE Development, and so on. Once these strategic business units are formed, the CEO then determines the few key activities needed to coordinate these lines of business. These activities, such as finance, planning, public affairs and shareholder relations are sometimes referred to as integrating mechanisms.

These decisions about the allocations of people can be the toughest. The loneliest moment the CEO experiences is usually when he must make a decision concerning someone's career. Decisions regarding who will stay, who will go or who will be advanced on the management team are not suitable for committee consideration. Michel Bélanger of The National Bank of Canada reported:

> The thing I find unpleasant is firing people. I've had to settle the resignation or assessment of a number of presidents and general managers. I find it tough to try explain to somebody that he is no damn good to the organization.

Jean de Grandpré of Bell Canada Enterprises discussed this difficult aspect of the CEO's job:

> I suppose it's dealing with people. Once you have the assets in place, then you have to manage them. You have to find the right people. I've always said that, when you deal with a piece of hardware, if you push a button the same light will always come up. But when you push the same button on fifteen different people, you will have fifteen different lights. What some think is great others will think is lousy. Managing people is probably the most difficult part of my job.

Chief executive officers will sometimes quietly admit they are uncomfortable with committees, that they prefer to deal on a one-on-one basis or a one-on-two basis. De Grandpré was asked if he worked with a group of management committees. "Oh, it's a lot easier to do it one-on-one. I can grab the phone and talk to them [my CEO and top people] and discuss important issues with them."

Other reasons to avoid committees often reflect the mythology of committees, which holds that if there is a difficult or roundabout way to do something, a committee will find it. Over the years, committees have also gained a reputation for being counterproductive. Others avoid committees because they perceive themselves as strong leaders and do not feel they need help making decisions. So, no committees.

Laurent Beaudoin, CEO of Bombardier, explained his preference for a one-on-one approach.

> Each of the divisions has its own management committee, which meets once a month. The division head reports to the group president who answers to me. When the group president has a problem and wants to talk to me, he comes in and we talk about it. A full review of the division's operations is done twice a year. Once I have approved the operating plan establishing profitability and growth, it is the group president who takes over and really monitors the division's performance. He works with them on a regular basis and I sit down with him on a monthly basis.

Even so, there are key issues that require team discussion, and CEOs are currently making far greater use of their management committee—that group of key executives who get together on a regular basis to coordinate and resolve interfunctional problems. Often such a committee will be limited to only those executives who report directly to the CEO. Some CEOs prefer an even smaller core-management committee, particularly if their span of management is quite broad. Other CEOs like to bring in key advisors from a number of levels of management. In all cases the committee structure acts as a formal mechanism for creating a forum for information-sharing, discussion and, on occasion, decision-making.

The use of committees is growing partly because of the complexities of business that create management issues which require expertise from more than one department in the corporation. A second reason lies in the CEO's recognition that committees help managers build teams that work well together and that ultimately help him in his leadership role. Raymond Cyr discusses his management style when he was leading Bell Canada before he moved on to become president of Bell Canada Enterprises:

> I am more the consensus type. We have a group of four executive VPs and myself. We form what we call the execu-

tive officer group, which meets twice a month to review a
number of things—from a new business acquisition to set-
tling on labor disputes or whatever. In a large corporation, I
have always felt that consensus, not unanimity, is important. If something does come up where we don't have a
consensus but which I feel we ought to be doing, then I will
simply let the thing simmer for a while. Eventually the
consensus does build up either for or against. Even though
people may feel that I make all the decisions, my feeling,
and that of those that have worked with me, is that we
have made very few decisions that were not supported by
the executive group.

There is no one model for a top management committee.
Indeed, that is one of the beauties of the mechanism: no
two committees work the same way. Flexibility is one of
the committee's strengths. What it is set up to do and how
it will function can be left to the personal preference of the
man who creates it—the chief executive officer. Allan
Taylor, CEO of the Royal Bank of Canada, uses a six-person
executive committee:

> It's not a decision-making body. It's what I use to bounce
> around the ideas that a colleague brings to me for a deci-
> sion. I'll say to him, "I want you to tell the committee today
> about what it is we're planning, and he'll outline roughly
> what there is, what the parameters of money [are], what we
> expect to get out of it. There's no question of power, be-
> cause these six people are in fact running the bank.

Most CEOs use their top management committee for certain
routine matters. It is a convenient forum at which each
member can highlight events in his particular sphere of influence, and voice an opinion on the new strategic plan
and the operating budget. Results can be regularly referred
to, and comments elicited from members on performance
planning. In addition, new product or service innovations
can be tested for senior management reaction, and new
personnel policies can be reviewed.

Some chief executive officers will rigidly limit their committees to such routine matters. They feel more comfortable

in dealing with these more predictable matters, and they have confidence in their ability to lead such discussions.

But more frequently, these routine matters are given limited time during the committee meeting. Most top management committees don't work to a rigid agenda; instead, they allow freewheeling discussion of important matters. Chief executive officers who make maximum use of their top management committees freely put these issues on the table for discussion so they can elicit a range of information and response. They expect their committee members to help set out the options so they can make the right decisions.

Richard Thomson, CEO of Toronto-Dominion Bank, uses the collegial style of management:

> When we go to a meeting we sit at a round table; everybody at that meeting is treated as an equal, no matter what level you're at, and we encourage different levels to come to a meeting. We encourage direct communication without going through various levels. We're called a flat organization and we'll jump levels. We don't respect titles for communication purposes.

Lorne Lodge, former CEO of IBM Canada, comments on IBM's use of meetings as forums at which younger managers can display their talent.

> [At committee meetings] I get exposed to an awful lot of people, not just those one level down from the committee members but frequently those about six levels down, who are at the meeting because that particular area is that person's speciality. Some presentations are well done but some presentations are so poorly done that people get into trouble and have to come back. I think it really teaches them something. And it gives me great exposure to them.

The top committee offers the leader an excellent way to assess his top team members. André Charron, former CEO of Lévesque, Beaubien, discussed the importance of this.

> I never worked without the executive committee or at least the top people in our organization. They would never

make a decision without consulting me. I would never make a decision without consulting them. If I pick them, it's because I want to work with them. I know that an executive who controls the company is there for a limited time. Yet the corporation will survive. And you've got to make sure your successor is there at all times.

Leaders also use committees to sort through the arguments that arise between line and staff management. Having a formal forum, where carefully led debate can be carried out between differing factions, gives the CEO a powerful insight into how each individual copes with interrelationships, both in relaxed discussion and during stressful confrontation. In short, committees are a living management-assessment laboratory.

Many CEOs regard their top committee as an important vehicle for implementing their personal style. People in organizations watch the boss. Therefore, they are going to notice the people he names to the committee. A new appointment signals the arrival of the new contender. Once on the committee, members will watch the leader carefully and listen to his every word. As chairman, the CEO can direct discussions, thereby creating an informal flow of information that will give him insight into what's going on throughout the corporation. Committees facilitate decision-making without removing the CEO's ultimate authority to make the important calls as he sees fit.

Robert Morison, CEO of Consumers Packaging, said:

> You can do nothing about today except be interested in what your people are doing from day to day. I've always said that the truly effective times of a CEO probably amount to about five or six hours a month. So what does a CEO do in my terms? What's his job? We recognize he can't influence today, tomorrow, next week or next month. He can influence three months from now if he rushes. When you get to six months out, beyond that, then the CEO's contribution becomes something that you can measure.

What Morison suggests is that those below the CEO are the ones making the decisions on day-to-day operations. The

CEO's impact on these operations takes a little time before it is felt. The plans are set, operations are in motion. The CEO is left to deal with the longer-range problems and decisions and that's a lonely ordeal.

We came across a dramatic instance of loneliness a number of years ago. One particular president had been encouraged to establish a top executive committee to begin to break down what had been high brick walls between key organizational functions. Everyone, however, underestimated the great discomfort this man had dealing with groups of more than two or three people. Unsure of his own knowledge and ability, he controlled the agenda so tightly that no subject could be introduced without his approval. He wanted varied opinions and information, but lacked the confidence to chair the meeting.

The result was predictable: three or four uninteresting rigid meetings, followed by a hiatus of some months before the next meeting. The only reason the next meeting was held was that the president was once again reminded of the need for such a group. It was the last time. He was left to make the key decisions alone, and as a result they were rarely made, if ever.

By contrast, we know a chief executive officer whose qualities of intelligence and experience are coupled with an insatiable love of his job. He works six days a week, fourteen hours a day. He not only knows his business and studies the facts, but he has the qualities of leadership that allow others to be both happy and confident with his decisions.

He could but doesn't make those decisions alone. Rather, he has established a management committee that works, because he makes it work. He ensures that its members come with the facts. He demands excellence in standards of reporting by being sure he has thought out and properly documented any issues he plans to introduce.

He forces participation as an automatic reaction. How? By having, over time, developed an attitude that each committee member must comment on every subject. And he has done that by never failing to ask each person's opinion on each issue.

He gets commitment to action by asking for it. And if it's not freely forthcoming, he will go back and rework the problem until the solution gains the committee's dedicated support.

He demands teamwork from the committee members. He is sensitive to each member's personality, his or her strengths and weaknesses. He often pairs members to form a task force to look more deeply into unresolved issues. Not infrequently, he chooses two disparate advocates. Ultimately they have to return with a conclusion to which they are both committed.

Above all, this leader demonstrates participation in decision-making by showing respect for the deliberations of his committee. Once having made his decision with committee expertise, or allowed the decision to be taken by consensus, he will stand by it.

The individual shapes the dynamics. As another example, Lorne Lodge expressed his style while CEO of IBM:

> There are five of us [on the operating review committee] and every function of the company is represented. We meet regularly. Everybody has an opportunity to contribute to any issue at all. They can agree, they can disagree, they know [that] because they all do it. I don't care whether the subject matter happens to be completely out of their bailiwick, they are part of the senior management of this company and I expect them to be aware and involved and to lend common sense to the issue. When a decision is taken they all know what the decision is and why it is taken. We all move out of one of those meetings and implement together. I have a little bit bigger vote. When I decide what I want to do, I am very comfortable that I have heard all sides.

Today there is a growing recognition that only by bringing the best management minds together can a CEO deal with increasingly complex top management issues. A confident CEO can gain much from sharing strategic decision-making with a carefully selected small executive team on an ongoing basis. Executive teams also offer the senior executives an excellent opportunity to familiarize themselves with the full range of problems facing a contemporary organization, and to prepare for the top job.

CHAPTER

9

THE BOARD
OF
DIRECTORS

In his book *Managing*, Harold Geneen begins his critique of boards of directors of the top five hundred industrial corporations in America with these words: "Above the exalted Chief Executive, if you look closely, is a large amorphous mass, representing the owners of the corporation, the stockholders. . .and if you look more closely, you will see that the mass of owners is connected to the corporate professional by an archaic, creaking contraption at the top called the 'Board of Directors'."

But what exactly is this creaking contraption? It is a group of considerable importance and it is legally accountable in many situations. The directors acting as a board are agents of the company for all purposes, and the shareholders are entitled to expect that the board will exercise its authority diligently. The board has not only the power, but the duty to manage the company.

Although the board cannot delegate its decision-making powers, it can give officers of the company certain responsibilities for the day-to-day conduct of the company's affairs. It is in this way that the chief executive officer receives his mandate to manage on behalf of the board of directors.

Then the question is, who manages whom? William Richards, former CEO of Dome Petroleum, said, "Poor old boards, they can't do a hell of a lot. They have to make decisions on the basis of what management tells them. They're a bit of a captive."

In theory, directors delegate responsiblity to others at their own risk. It is not easy, as reflected in the comments of Irving Ludmer of Steinberg Inc.:

> The board has to evaluate how much freedom they give the CEO. Real-estate types like me sometimes will take enormous risks, a là Bob Campeau with Allied Stores. We are comfortable with high leverage and so on, but how does a board accept this sort of thing when it wants to keep the debt-equity ratio at a comfortable 35:65? How do boards react to outside experts putting out statements that market share should be this, and return on equity that, and return on investment capital this? If a CEO does this he is considered a great manager. But what does the board do with a guy who says he wants return on equity as high as possible? The analysts get nervous. When they ask what market share I want, and I say, "Well, a lineup on the sidewalk outside every store and the fire marshall saying that it's okay to let two more in—that's market share." I don't say numbers aren't important, but they are a way of keeping score. They don't make business. They never will make business.

There is, however, some help for the board members. The Canadian federal government and the provincial governments allow a director to rely in good faith on the "financial statements of the corporation represented to him by an officer of the corporation or in a written report of the auditor of the corporation fairly to reflect the financial condition of the corporation." Directors may also rely on certain persons whose profession lends credibility to their respective opinions, such as chartered accountants and lawyers.

Beyond its legal obligations the board of directors has, among others, the following duties:

- It selects the chief executive officer and the principal members of the management team;
- It insists that management is properly structured and that it has a clear definition of the mission and directions to be taken by the company;
- It is accountable for the financial performance of the corporation;
- It considers the impact of the actions of the corporation on the society of which it is a part;
- It sees that policies and procedures are in place to promote compliance with the laws governing the corporation; and it establishes proper standards of performance to measure top management performance.

In short, the directors must take care of management succession, watch over performance, be considerate of the corporation's place and contribution to society and be sure that the corporation complies with government rules and regulations.

Accomplishing all these tasks is a heavy order, especially in the face of two important facts. The first is that today boards of directors must understand the uncertain and volatile changes in external markets. And second, boards of directors are dependent on management to provide the information and understanding they need to perform their duties. Let's look at these two facts.

Thirty years ago, boards of directors exercised their authority with great confidence—confidence in their choice of officers and in the officers' knowledge, and confidence in their own abilities to arrive at appropriate decisions. Their responsibilities were less than those of today's directors, but their working environment was more predictable, just as it was for the officers who were accountable to them.

Thirty years ago, shareholders for the most part were members of the middle and upper classes. Even institutional shareholders were often passive and friendly. On the whole the economic times were good, except for brief recessionary doldrums such as the slump that followed the Korean War. In spite of the occasional blip in performance, most boards of directors were happy with the activities of their corporations.

But times have changed. Businesses are more complex; customers are more demanding; competitors are more aggressive as markets stabilize; financing has become more sophisticated; international factors, such as foreign currency fluctuations, can affect corporate performance; government regulation is increasingly difficult. All these changes make board members feel less in control today than they once were.

In addition, directors have, in recent years, discovered that their responsibilities are not just to the shareholders, the creditors, the employees and the government, but also to the public at large. Society is speaking out when the actions of public companies affect the environment and working and living conditions.

Given all these new factors, it is essential that boards of directors, most of whose members are part-time, get the information they need to make wise judgments.

Today more than ever, directors realize they must rely on their appointed managers for information. The flow of data from the managerial level to the board is essential if they are to protect themselves and the well-being of their company.

The truth is that much of what directors learn is from what management tells them. The extent to which a board is fully apprised of events—strategies, plans and performance—is in large part the foundation of its ability to do what it is responsible for: overseeing and evaluating the performance of the very individuals who give them the data.

Yet most board members recognize that the messages they are sent are invariably optimistic. Whatever the results, management often tends to report favorably on how well the company is doing despite a negative economy or a slack market. As one veteran board member put it: "Management never admits that they have done a sloppy job or that they were outsmarted by competitors.

They always have a rationale to defend what didn't happen."

For this reason boards of public companies are placing increasing importance on their audit committees. A strong audit committee is usually comprised of outside directors, independent of the chairman and CEO. This committee, in most cases, provides the board with a real degree of independence from management, since it brings to the board the objective and independent opinions of the company's external auditors. Indeed, more boards are using the external auditor as more than an independent accounting auditor; they are creating a special role, that of independent managing auditor. This move is evidence of an increased desire by concerned boards for facts independent of those provided by the management over which they must sit in judgement. Additional independence can be created by constituting an executive committee of the board whose chairman is an independent outside director and whose members would also be outsiders, with the exception of the CEO.

But at the same time as the boards' need for knowledge based on hard facts has increased, there are the added difficulties of infrequent meetings (sometimes only four times a year) and outside directors who know little about the day-to-day operations. These compound the problem. The liabilities of directors are increasing, and with those increased liabilities is the need to get closer to, and be more aware of, what is going on in the business. The day has gone when, as one CEO wryly stated, "a board could have peace and tranquility, no surprises and no embarrassments."

There are those who suggest that in today's complex business environment, many boards of directors have not adequately fulfilled their role—judging management's competence. Some critics say that boards must demand stronger management performance if Canadian corporate productivity is to be substantially improved. There is also criticism of the fact that Canadian corporate directorships are so intertwined, so incestuous even—that far too frequently the same faces greet each other across the oval tables in different boardrooms. Many of these individuals were, or are, themselves chief executive officers who in turn will face some of their boardroom associates at their next board meeting. In this situation some do not probe too deeply, or ask too many embarrassing questions, or be too demanding. It is just not the correct thing to do. Besides, boards of directors rarely challenge the performance of the chief executive officer. In the past, when a challenge arose, this delicate affair was often left to a small committee of the board. Frequently, such committees lacked the proper knowledge with which to measure performance.

Many CEOs we have talked with felt that their boards' measure of their success was based more on personal evaluation or conclusions than on sound factual judgment. Some of them questioned the degree of diligence and accountability demanded of them by their respective boards.

Such sloppiness on the part of the board leads to mediocre performance and disastrous results. Even when some major Canadian corporations were continually showing declining results, the boards made no change in their corporate leadership.

It has been said that if a major company is in trouble, the chances are that not only has its management been inadequate to meet the challenges, but that its board of directors has not done its job. In reality, the two go together. You cannot have a successful, growing and dynamic corporation unless it blends the strengths of its board of directors with that of its management. They are irrevocably drawn together. As Kenneth Dayton, former chairman of the board of directors of Dayton Hudson, once said: "Corporate governance and corporate management are two sides of the same coin. You can't for long have one without the other."

When examining the relationship between a board of directors and its chief executive officer, we found that a variety of relationships exists due to the variety in the structure of boards. For example, there are boards of directors of mutual life assurance companies where the widely dispersed multitude of policyholders are in fact the shareholders. Board members who represent these individual policyholders are carefully selected and put forward by a nominating committee from the existing board. Rarely are these selections—selections the CEO normally concurs with—not approved at the annual meeting.

A different structure exists where substantial minority interests win representation on a public company's board of directors. These representatives are appointed by the minority shareholders and are there to represent their interests, sometimes more in an adversarial than partnership relationship to the rest of the board of directors.

Another variety of structure is based on a tradition of having, along with the chief executive officer, other management team members on the board of directors—thus creating the inside and outside director syndrome.

Maurice Jodoin, CEO of General Trustco, described some desired fundamental changes in the nature of membership of boards of directors:

> With all the complexities of business today, a director cannot simply be involved to the extent of a half day four or five times a year. There well may be a requirement for more full-time directors who are more actively involved in the companies, where you are looking for a combination of senior management and more leadership in the company. A board may not be effective if it is made up of people who are doing it on a very fragmented and minimal part-time basis.

There are further variations on the theme, but suffice to say that the relationship between the board and its CEO largely begins with the membership structure of the board. A board's membership sets the climate within which the board exercises its power to appoint and dismiss the CEO, or to give or take away levels of authority.

The structure also dictates the degree to which members are truly independent of management. The whole issue of board independence is coming to the fore as boards come under close public scrutiny. David McCamus of Xerox described the situation.

> What's happened is that the hired hands and the proprietors have become sort of mushed up. But there

should be a difference between the proprietor and the hired hands, and that's where we've lost a certain amount of the natural role of the board, to maintain that sort of tension between the two.

Probably the most debated point is whether the chairman of the board should also be the corporation's CEO. In such cases, the president becomes the chief operating officer. This is something of a tradition in the United States and can be seen in the structure of three-fourths of the Fortune 500 corporations. Traditionally in major European corporations, the chairman is rarely the top paid executive. But, in the United Kingdom, there has been a gradual trend to appointing an executive chairman who is also the CEO, and the managing director has become the chief operating officer. The Canadian situation, which for many years reflected a preference for the president as CEO, has begun to move in the same direction as the United States, with the chairman as CEO.

The issue of independence between the board and management becomes more relevant when you consider who the chief executive officer is. Deference to the board is more evident in situations where the chairman is not the CEO. When the chairman is the CEO, that person has more power. He manages not only the board, but the company. He also has the opportunity to exercise great control because he can influence the selection of the directors who will ultimately sit in judgement of him.

CEOs themselves are divided on the issue of whether it is fair to the stockholders when a corporation has its CEO as chairman.

Purdy Crawford, CEO of Imasco, addressed the question:

It is surprising how split people are on their views as to whether the chairman of the board should at the same time be the CEO of the corporation. If you go into law and into directorship responsibilities and see what is delegated to directors, it is hard to see how they can carry out their functions if they are led in the activity by the same person whose performance they should be evaluating. On the other hand, you get guys asking how you can be chairman of a major corporation and carry out any function unless you have an intimate knowledge of the corporation—unless you are, in effect, the CEO. They say they can do a better job of keeping their board informed of what's going on because they are CEO. Interesting arguments! If you are chairman and CEO, in some ways the board becomes more your creature than you are a creature of the board, and that does not help.

Some advocate removing the CEO and any internal management from membership on the board to give directors independence and freedom to carry out their responsibility of reviewing management's performance. Others point to the fact that accountability for the corporation's policies and actions is falling more heavily on boards of directors. They say there are limits to the abilities of a part-time chairman. Thus, some boards prefer to keep the ultimate powers of the chief executive officer (including control of information) in their own hands by designating it to their leader—the chairman. Richard Thomson believes:

> If you're the chairman and you're going to keep your board fully informed, the only way you're going to know that you're keeping your board fully informed is to be very informed yourself; the most informed person should be the chief executive officer, and therefore, I feel I am in the best position to make sure our board is fully informed.

The combined CEO-chairman structure reaffirms the belief of those who think that the chairman of the board is ultimately the man who carries the can. It is he who must ultimately answer for the poor performance of the board and the corporation. Since this is the case, why not give him the title of CEO as well?

Sir David Orr, former chairman of Unilever, suggested that this trend is due to the fact that accountability—to shareholders, particularly institutions, to know what is going on in the company—has made it desirable for the man who is the major decision-taker also to be the man who steps up and takes accountability.

Indeed, if one returns to the legal definition of a director's role and that of boards of directors, it is clear that the board has not only the power but the duty to manage the corporation. In that context, it would seem that a chairman can certainly warrant being the CEO.

Edward Crawford, Chairman, President and CEO of Canada Life, said that his combined roles provided him with an important advantage because of his knowledge of company operations and objectives.

> I believe the concept of an outside chairman will become extinct. The outsider has a very difficult role. He may not have the insight into the company's affairs because he is not there all the time. It's like having a queen and a prime minister in a business. It doesn't work.

Michael Cornelissen, the young, dynamic CEO of Royal Trust, argued the other side. He is convinced that the role of the CEO must be separated from that of chairman. He believes that the chairman has a different set of accountabilities from the CEO. The board under the leadership of the chairman has four responsibilities: first, to safeguard shareholders' values; second, to select and evaluate the CEO; third, to review vigorously and approve the annual strategic plan of the organization; and fourth, to ensure they receive all the information they require to carry out the first three roles.

There are other reasons for separating the positions. Robert Kadlec, CEO of Inland Natural Gas said:

> First there is a natural synergy when the CEO and the chairman discuss issues, whether they relate to policy, compensation or sales. There is also the opportunity for a CEO to share the pressures. The CEO has someone to turn to and the chairman can help you a lot with the board because he can get the communication links with members. The greater the conversation at the board level, the stronger the company is going to be.

Often preferences are dictated by the owner relationship. Brascan's CEO, Trevor Eyton, explained his corporate preference.

We feel that as a major shareholder in the company we
have a special right to name the chairman, who ideally
should not be the chief executive officer. We think the
chairman should particularly represent the whole of the
board and the shareholders through them.

On the other side are the hired professionals like Robert
Gratton of Montreal Trust:

When you have controlling shareholders and the CEO is not
the chairman, then the chairman, because he deals with the
controlling shareholders, becomes a source of power and
influence. This chairman now becomes much stronger and
is in potential conflict with the CEO, who also would like to
have this direct link with the controlling shareholder.

The arguments will understandably continue. In the
meantime, a special onus of responsibility must be borne
by the chairman who also carries the responsibility of CEO.
On the one hand, as chairman, he must optimize the role of
the board to encourage discussions, questions, challenges
and, hopefully, criticisms. Above all, he must ensure that
the board expects management to excel. As CEO, he must
present and sell his plans and programs to achieve solid
goals. He must be accountable. Jean de Grandpré of Bell
Canada Enterprises discussed accountability in the context
of the chairman and CEO issue:

Quite frankly, I think the problem is exaggerated in terms
of importance, or in terms of conflicts, or in terms of objec-
tivity. The chief executive officer is answerable to the board,
but he is also answerable to the shareholders, and if he
doesn't do his job and the board doesn't act, he will not be
able to hold on—the shareholders' pressure will be such
that the board will have to act.

Recently, boards of directors have begun to function more
effectively. Their members are becoming increasingly
aware of their liabilities and the absolute need for
diligence. With this awareness there is also a greater understanding that the board, when such performance is
found to be inadequate, must do something about it.

In talking to chief executive officers we found that effective boards of directors are those that place certain demands on their chief executive officers. Among the things boards should demand are the following:

- A statement of mission for the company that clearly outlines what businesses the organization is in and also, what business it should not be in;
- A measure of management's performance against board-approved plans and objectives;
- Assurance that management is properly structured and adequately staffed and that careful management succession plans are laid out;
- Evidence of the adequacy of management information systems and effective accounting contacts;
- Accurate, timely information for the board itself.

As we have mentioned, the most important job the board of directors has is that of assessing management's performance. To perform this task properly the board must ensure that the board committee in charge of the evaluation process is independent of the chairman if he is also the CEO. This committee must avoid focusing only on whether the CEO is carrying out the various duties written in his job description. Its members must judge also whether his leadership has allowed the company to continue to achieve its goals in a sustained manner over a number of years. They need to be able to measure the corporation's improved operating performance. They need to be confident that the CEO has a sense of how far the company can go in its future directions. This should not be an annual event. It should be an ongoing appraisal, which regularly keeps score of financial performance, market growth and position, product or service leadership, depth of management and people skills, relationships with its public and the soundness of future direction and planning, including discussions on management succession.

Robert Martin, CEO of Consumers' Gas, recognized that his board has a responsibility to assess management performance.

I accept and believe that the principle of responsibility is to be the agent of shareholders. They should be monitoring me and putting me to whatever tests they think are reasonable to assure themselves that the place is being run well now and long-term. Having said that, if they're a good board, then they should be used by me. I should be able to get some meaningful feedback from them. I should get input on issues that are important to the company. I don't want them sitting on their hands. And I would expect that I could use them individually if I needed contacts or help or whatever.

The truest test of a board's ability to be independent and to honor its obligations and duties to the shareholders is its system for judging management's performance and for rewarding the performance of its senior executives. In the truly successful enterprise, one normally finds a board of directors that has rigorously exercised this function. Its chief executive officer's primary role is the management of the company on behalf of the board. A CEO who recognizes this will allow his board to carry out its role—to urge excellence—because such a CEO recognizes that his actions will in turn create excellence in management.

CHAPTER

10

GOVERNMENT

The world in which the corporation competes is a diverse one. The CEO is expected to interpret this world to his organization, and to speak to the many "publics" that have an impact on the organization—shareholders, key suppliers, prime customers, labor groups, the financial community, industry groups and, of course, government. Rarely today can any major corporation move to make significant change without having to deal with at least one level of government. Because of this, and because governments in Canada are so intertwined in our business life, we have devoted a chapter to the subject of the CEO and government.

When he was CEO of Crowntek Communications Donald Wood said:

> We are going to need as much leadership in twenty years as we do now and we did twenty years ago. There will be changes. Obviously, government involvement is going to increase, so in addition to communicating with your board you are going to have to communicate with politicians and civil servants. There are a lot of industries that are already like that: Air Canada, Bell, all those guys are up to their

ears in it. When you consider that there are certain people who like to do that and who are better at it, they will more likely be the CEOs of the future.

Expectations in Canadian society are constantly changing, and society has increasingly turned to government for the realization of those expectations, thus placing new demands on the business community and challenging many of its traditional assumptions.

Among the things that Canadian expect their governments to provide are the following:

Financial security now and in the future

Financial security implies adequate income for the unemployed, the injured, the handicapped, the ill and the elderly. It also implies that funds invested in insurance, retirement plans and banks be insured so that the investor will not lose a life's savings should the institution fail.

Quality of work life

Employees expect safe, healthy working conditions, adequate compensation for the work performed, vacations, sick leave, maternity leave and a limit on the actual hours that must be worked.

A safe environment

An increasing awareness of the dangers of pollution has created a demand for clean air, clean water and safe disposal of toxic wastes.

Human rights

Legislation on human rights is continually expanding, and includes laws to ensure that hiring practices do not discriminate on the basis of race, creed, religion, sex, sexual orientation or against the handicapped (assuming they can actually perform the work). It is expanding to include freedom from sexual harassment, equal pay for work of e-qual value (to ensure equality of salary between men and women) and what are called affirmative-action hiring programs. These programs are slightly different than hiring quotas, which compel the employer to hire a certain number of people from specific racial groups or from a specific sex. Affirmative-action programs require employers to reserve a certain number of positions for specific racial or sexual groups and train the members of those groups to fill the positions.

Consumer expectations
People want to know what products are made of, or with; they want quality of manufacturing and they expect safety of use.

Health expectations
Health expectations go further than consumer expectations to ensure that the ingredients are safe and that the product is constructed safely. Although these expectations or demands on the part of the citizenry may be quite reasonable, they have nonetheless resulted in major adjustments in the business world because, more often than not, governments have eagerly taken up the cause and created new regulations to meet the public's desires. These regulations must be adhered to , and how the CEO copes with this new business reality while keeping the company profitable is a measure of his performance.

Moreover, within the corporate organization itself, attitudes have changed. Those inside the organization who want change but do not expect it to occur as a result of internal decisions also turn to the legislative process for support. More creative jobs, greater security in those jobs, improved working conditions, more generous benefits, shorter work hours—these are expectations that if not forthcoming from within, need a force from without. In many cases it simply means going to the government.

Paralleling the growth of the myriad government regulations is the general public's growing lack of confidence in the business community, big business in particular. The average person distrusts big business and has little good to say about the motives of its leaders. Those who lead major public companies are perceived as greedy egotists who have little regard for their employees or the public at large. This impression is fueled by the news of plant closures and layoffs and reports of executive salaries and bonuses that figure in the hundreds of thousands of dollars, of handsome stock options and of the golden handshakes representing generous separation payments for those who don't succeed. All these have led to more cynicism about the titans of big business.

Our governments do little to combat the poor impression of big business in the eyes of the public. There is the occasional bland statement of support of potential job creation by major corporate enterprise, but it is far more politically popular to be seen standing somewhat apart fom big business. It is more popular yet to be seen to step in and to regulate what big business does.

When a major corporate disaster occurs, and in recent years there have been several in our financial service sector, government moves quickly to establish a special investigation of the companies involved. Such investigations are a precursor to yet more regulation, which seeks to assure the avoidance of a similar occurrence in the future.

Corporations are being held not only morally responsible but legally liable for their actions in this increasingly complex external environment. Given this environment, it is not surprising that the chief executive officer has come to realize that no significant decision can be made in his corporation without taking governmental realities into account.

Be it in manufacturing and production, product research and quality, marketing and distribution, pricing, advertising, personnel policies, diversification or export or import, there are regulations by levels of government.

The late Val Stock, when CEO of Canada Packers, looked back:

> When I was younger, maybe I didn't pay that much attention to the public sector. The federal government was something out there that did a few little services for us but they didn't regulate what we were doing or have any real control over what we were doing. That has certainly changed—just dramatically. So today there's less freedom to run

your business on the basis that you want to run it because
of all this interference from government.

The cost of dealing with government regulations in terms
of hours of effort, dollars spent on forms and administration, lost opportunity and so on are astronomical. It has
simply become another fixed cost of doing business, and is
in the end passed on to the very people whose expectations initiated it all in the first place—the consumers.

All our interviews have shown that one of the most
difficult ongoing issues Canadian chief executive officers
believe they must deal with is the impact of government
on their enterprise. It probably represents their most
frustrating issue, as well, for few of them know how to
cope with it effectively.

Few CEOs know a great deal about what government
really is and does, how it is organized, how decisions are
made and what makes elected officials and civil servants
tick. They have at best a grudging respect and at worst a
total distain for the public-service sector.

The corporate leader knows that he thinks differently from
senior civil servants and that he works under a very different
set of formal rules. Those rules make it tough for the two
sides to work together. One is bottom-line or result-oriented,
the other process-oriented. Peter Drucker, in his book *The
Changing Work of the Executive*, stresses this point:

> The first job of the executive is to make his organization
> perform. Results are always on the *outside*. There are only
> costs on the inside. Even the most efficient manufacturing
> plant is still a cost center until a distant customer has paid
> for its products. The executive thus lives in a constant
> struggle to keep performance from being overtaken by the
> concerns of the inside, that is by the bureaucracy.

Major corporate enterprises must constantly respond to
opportunities and problems presented by the market and
are judged on their market performance and profitability.
On the other hand, the public service does not have to
respond to the market. Government leaders such as
cabinet ministers and ministers' deputies cannot measure

performance of their often large and complex departments and agencies in the marketplace. Instead they have an unenviable task: to attempt to manage a large, ponderous bureaucratic process. Trying to introduce an element of entrepreneurship or results-oriented management is difficult indeed, and rarely, if ever, achieved in the public sector. Over time the leadership qualities of those in positions of governmental authority become markedly different from their counterparts of the corporate world. Their missions are different; their objectives rarely match; their standards of performance bear little resemblance nor do their management styles.

Speaking on relations with government, Purdy Crawford, CEO of Imasco, said, "I was more aware of insensitivity to government in my other environment. I used to say to clients, 'Look, you've got to put yourself in their shoes, you're not being reasonable from their perspective. But they would do upsetting little things, like calling them bureaucrats in their presence.'"

It is not surprising that government and industry leaders often do not understand each other. Businessmen come from a management system that rests on the principle that, according to Joseph Brown, "Managers should make the most efficient and effective use of the resources at their disposal. We measure organizations of this sort by results." Government leaders tend to "rest on the principle that managers should try to ensure that the system treats fairly most of the people it affects. We measure organizations of this type by the legitimizing of their internal processes and by the public accountability of their officers." (*Harvard Business Review*, July-August 1983.)

The result is that there are two solitudes, and members of both camps are suspicious of each others' motives and moves. As one former senior federal mandarin stated succinctly: "We must find a way to close a yawning chasm between Ottawa and so much of the business community. Our first objective must be to maintain an attitude of mutual respect."

Unquestionably, our findings suggest that many business executives support this wish. They recognize that, no matter how hard they may wish otherwise, government pervasiveness is here to stay. It is therefore smart business to move away from an adversarial position to a stance that encourages greater cooperation and understanding. Lou Hollander said: "The government is a bunch of people who have a job to do. If you go and talk to them and listen to them and find out where they are coming from, they can be an asset." More chief executive officers are finding that they need to devote more time to what they concede is the non-economic (or at least non-operational) side of their business. Trevor Eyton, CEO of Brascan, stated:

> Dealing with the government takes more and more time. Nonetheless, I have to say that in recent times there is both a public awareness and I think awareness among bureaucrats and politicians that the private sector has much to contribute.

Robert Kadlec, CEO of Inland Natural Gas, talked about building credibility and trust.

> Meeting government, telling government our story—I spend a lot of time on that. I think we're respected in Victoria, but it's because of one-on-one conversations like the one we're having. You have to keep going at it. People have got to realize that Bob Kadlec is an honest guy, and when he says he's going to do something, he'll perform. You only get that from performance and relating to people. I think that's one thing we've built up in British Columbia. Victoria knows that our company is an honest performer, a company that's out to do things for the province and become successful on the way.

Public policy is now a matter of serious study for the chief executive officer, and boards of directors are growing more sensitive to their organization's image in the community. They expect their executives to ensure that their enterprises are seen to be productive forces in the communities they serve.

So in Canada today to a far greater degree than we can remember we see executive leaders spending more time and effort working at the problem of trying to improve the confidence of the public in business. They are doing so in different ways but all are attempting to build greater goodwill and reduce consumers' criticisms.

Edward Crawford, CEO of Canada Life, has been a participant in various government commissions and study groups. His view illustrates a tolerance toward rules and regulations.

> By definition we have to be aware of the regulatory problems of every jurisdiction in which we operate. We need to know when governments pass legislation that affects us—if not directly, then indirectly. Part of the job today is to try to see what can be done to make that legislation workable.

The advice between this experienced CEO's lines is clear. The corporation's aim should be to provide information that will lead to workable legislation.

Rowland Frazee, former CEO of the Royal Bank of Canada, states his approach to the relationship between government and the business community.

> Some people will say that chief executives have to spend more time being aware of the government because governments spend a lot of time being aware of the business community. I don't know whether that's a change or not. I think if you leave national issues to the politicians and you don't like what comes out, you've only got yourselves to blame. That's why I've always been prepared to make speeches addressing national issues. I think that's the role of the CEO. Call it a lobby or whatever, you've got to establish yourself with the government.

The Business Council on National Issues began a decade ago, and today represents a large segment of the country's major corporations. It brings together highly dedicated business leaders to discuss, debate, research and formulate business opinion. The results are given to top government officials and often affect their policy deliberation. Those who belong to the Business Council on National Issues understand that a strong corporate business system will simply not survive if the public perceives it to be against its best interests. Through their collective and individual actions, these executives are attempting, out of corporate interest, to supply quality goods and services, and to be fair employers and reasonable corporate citizens.

There are a number of approaches that executives in major public organizations may take to become more involved in and aware of the public sector. First, they can study the organization of government and, in particular, its decision-making process. They are frequently surprised to find how different it is from what they are accustomed to. In government the process is complex and full of checks and balances, and it requires paperwork and explanations that from a businessman's point of view bear little relevance to the decision to be made.

Frustration often develops when proposals from business to government are turned down even though they clearly forecast performance results that would meet the most stringent guidelines of the most exacting of boards of directors. The problem is simply that the executives involved do not quite understand the government decision-making process. Knowledgeable chief executive officers learn how to use the government system to their advantage. They understand the importance of the civil service and they give the bureaucracy the facts it needs, using the government's measurement system of cost benefit to the community. Lynton Wilson, CEO of Redpath Industries, a former deputy minister of industry and tourism for the Ontario government, explains how he uses his knowledge of government:

> I can understand the forces at play when the government is faced with a certain kind of decision: the pressures, the policy papers, the political side. I can understand what's likely to be the outcome when an issue is up for grabs better than my colleagues who haven't had my experience in government. They tend to be more dogmatic.

The chief executive officers who are successful in dealing with government have done their homework. Whether they are to appear before a parliamentary or legislative committee, or be part of a group of executives making a brief, or meeting to discuss the potential re-zoning of an important parcel of land with key municipal officials, they insist that careful study take place before the fact. They ask: Who will be there? What are their motivations? What are the current regulations? Is what we propose stated in language that meets these needs? Have we all the facts?

The knowledgeable chief executive officer often takes the time to walk the corridors of the legislative or par-liamentary buildings to gain a sense of the climate and the atmosphere. He frequently establishes a new public or governmental affairs department within his organization to monitor, analyze and identify the impact of governmen-tal actions on his organization, and to ensure that the in-formation is available to help form the directions and ob-jectives within his strategic planning process. Alternatively he might contract consultants who specialize in govern-ment.

Before he succeeded Paul Paré as CEO of Imasco, Purdy Crawford was a highly competent corporate lawyer who had built up a solid record of effective communication with government. When asked what suggestions he had for his fellow CEOs when dealing with government, he replied:

> I would suggest first of all that, maybe not at their level, but someplace in the corporation, that they get an ongoing plan to see the public servants who are involved: the lower level first. Get to understand their concerns. Get a feel for what's driving them. And when you've got an understand-ing of what their objective is and what's driving them, then formulate how you're going to handle it based upon an understanding of the other side and how you're going to accommodate, in part or in whole, what you want to achieve. Your art has to be the art of compromise. [You have to] work out a solution that you can live with, that the people who answer to political constituencies can live with, and that the public servants who have ideas about public policy and responsibilities to their bosses can live with.

On the other side, government has also improved communications with business. To some extent government has reorganized its functions and activities to make it easier for the businessman to deal with them. Certainly in the past twenty years governments have sought out more spokespeople from the corporate community for consultation purposes. Proposed policies and programs that will affect the business community are now often communicated well before they become formal initiatives.

There are a number of important initiatives that government needs to make. The first is to consult the business sector in private consultations and before parliamentary committees. The second is to extend the use of executive exchange appointments, which draw outstanding individuals from both sides, and to support better use of advisory committees of executives.

No chapter on the interaction of Canadian government and Canadian chief executive officers can be written without some comment on Canadian Crown corporations—which are many and more varied in size, shape, administration and activity than most people would imagine. They straddle the fence between the private and public sectors. On the one hand, they often have a corporate form and are commercial in nature. Yet they are frequently subject to direction from government with respect to their policies. Thus they need to find the perfect mix between meeting commercial market demands and political realities.

Historically, with the obvious exception of transportation, not much competition existed between Crown corporations and public companies. But in the past twenty years this has changed dramatically and the likes of *Petro-Canada* have moved into the traditional sphere of public companies. Joint ventures with the private sector and other forms of administration have thrust new government initiatives into the market.

Thus far, Canadian corporate business executives have been critical of this phenomenon. They feel that it is tough enough to compete in today's market against aggressive competition, without having to compete against Crown corporations, which are seen to be protected from the true disciplines of marketplace performance, and which enjoy privileged positions because of their ownership. On the other hand, not too many would admit wanting to take on what they can see as the very complex and onerous task of trying to run one of those agencies.

The recent trend toward privatization, which is growing in popularity around the world and in Canada, may alleviate the problem. Yet the very nature of our society might suggest that what leaves will, in time, return to the public domain. The private sector will always have to live, however uneasily, with Crown corporations.

Government is into the world of business; it is in its political interests to be so. Governments will continue to have a pervasive influence on the growth of public corporations and their actions. We have found that the perceptive chief executive officer is therefore paying increasing attention to public policy and is encouraging his corporation to be more actively a part of the social political process. There is also among many a growing desire to influence government and to serve business interests as well. Government will not go away; it can no longer be ignored. But possibly a concerted effort by business and government leaders individually and collectively can help to check excess growth in, and exercise of, governmental power. There are many areas where voluntary compliance with certain public pressure is far better than mandatory adherence to regulatory laws.

Many CEOs quietly admit that the day of publicly criticizing government intervention while at the same time looking for government grants and favors has to end and be replaced by a more open and interactive dialogue. Canadian companies will need government cooperation to gain and sustain a reasonable share of world markets.

4

TOMORROW

Tomorrow's executives and tomorrow's CEOs will face greater challenges. In this chapter we explore the indicators of executive potential and the importance of strategic entrepreneurial spirit. We also consider the future challenges and opportunities presented by women executives. The corporate world of tomorrow will be very different from that of today. The exponential thrust of change will ensure that. The question is: will our CEOs measure up?

CHAPTER

11

PICKING
THE WINNERS

O ne of the board of directors' most important responsibilities is to identify and appoint the next CEO. So far in this book we have explored the development, abilities and attitudes of those individuals who have been successful in making it all the way to the top job in a corporation. Our observations have provided some ideas about what a board might profitably look for in those it is considering for the CEO appointment itself. We believe they apply equally well to the selection of "fast-trackers" at all management levels.

What are the success indicators of those who make it to the short lists and to eventual appointment?

Some Success Indicators

High intelligence
By intelligence we mean an amalgam of knowlege of the industry, the foresight and intelligence to identify problems and the will or the courage to take action. Gerry Hobbs, retired head of Cominco, said:

I think people are very much more able than they realize, given an opportunity and some help. Once they get going they really begin to take off like rockets. Really exciting to watch. I've thrown more people into the deep ends of pools than I can count, and I have yet to have one that didn't swim.

Early Demonstration Of Potential

Those who go far tend to start early. There are at least two reasons for this: first, an early start gives the person more experience in less time, and second, if the person is seen in a favorable light, he or she will come to the attention of more senior executives.

In discussing his early career with Canadian General Electric, William Blundell spoke of starting off in the air-conditioning group, which was not "on the main stream" at CGE.

One of the things that was good about it was that I learned that you had to make money in marketing. The first job was in sales, application and engineering. I started off in the company with a product line that was not great, and having to face the customers and all their complaints. I had a couple of years of very heavy front-end grassroots experience, which I think, in hindsight, was excellent in terms of really having to deal with an angry customer and sort out sticky affairs.

Few Obvious Flaws

There is considerable evidence that in evaluating others we give much more weight to negative qualities than to those that are positive. For this reason, any negative attributes (such as limited education, poor social skills, or poor appearance, experience in the wrong industry or in the wrong role) can cause an individual to be over-looked. Some studies suggest that negative characteristics carry seven times the weight of positive attributes. It isn't logical, but it is factual. Sometimes relatively minor negative attributes have overbalanced strong positive ones.

Experience In A Variety Of Functions

An individual who is a successful generalist clearly has the ability to advance beyond a functional specialty and become an effective CEO. On the other hand individuals who may have shone in a functional area such as finance, marketing or production, may not be capable of assuming the wider view. Thomas Galt, chairman and CEO of Sun Life Assurance of Canada, said:

> I am a great believer in a broad education. When I say broad, I mean taking an interest in the broader picture at the beginning rather than burying yourself too much in any one technically narrow sphere. Obviously human relations—how to deal with people—are vitally important, but it seems to me to be the one thing that gets left out of our educational system more than any other, but it is one of the most important.

The Ability To Cope With Stress And Adversity

As recruiters searching for individuals who can assume the top job, we look for a time in the person's career when things went wrong. It is easy to look good in a good economy, a growing industry and a healthy company, but not everyone can cope with the stress of adverse circumstances, and it is hard to predict who will be able to withstand stress while still being effective. No company wants a CEO who falls apart when the going gets tough and the company needs him the most! The individual's track record can be the best predictor of stress management. As one CEO put it: "The person we look for is cool under stress. That's one of the first things that you recognize in a person. Their ability to handle your questions, their ability to make their presentations."

The Ability To Deal With Mistakes, To Admit Them And To Go On With The Job

Every executive makes mistakes, and some of them may be major errors, but they need not be fatal. The degree to which a mistake affects a company will depend on the way the executive deals with it. Executives who feel they must be perfect and who try to cover up or bluff their way out of a mistake will not fool anyone. Nor will those who fail to correct their mistakes and get the company back on course.

David Clark, formerly an executive with Thomas Lipton Inc., now president and CEO of Campbell Soup Company, commented on his mistakes.

> I owe a lot to Lipton for my current success, because I was allowed, in the ten years there, through false starts and other things, to make a lot of mistakes that taught me important lessons. Then, when I hit the front door of Campbells's on March 26, 1983, I just ran.

A Positive View Of Others

The executive with a positive view of other groups or levels in the corporation will have greater effectiveness in building and maintaining a team. The tactful executive who is concerned with the self esteem of others will be able to develop loyalty in his staff.

Robert Hurlbut, chairman, formerly CEO of General Foods, said:

> I've seen some brilliant people, high performers, fall flat on their faces because they have been unable to communicate with people, their staff, their peers. They have been shoddy in their dealings with people. When you appoint someone to a general manager's job, this criterion would be right near the top. No one can do it himself, he has to do the job with people, and so people skills rank very very high up the list.

Donald McIvor, formerly chairman and CEO of Imperial Oil, commented on an executive who used interpersonal skills in a different way.

> I noticed that where some other executives were bouncing around, spending time repairing situations they had created, this fellow just sailed right through the whole thing. I asked him what he did, and he said, "I sit down and ask who are the chief actors in this issue, then I ask what is the key issue. This is not a value judgment about whether the conflict is right or wrong, but what is key to

each of those individuals. I know I need the support of each person. I will not give in on matters of principle but I will give way on other issues." He approaches the whole problem that way, and his work is better than others who do not take that approach.

Performance That Involves Sacrifice

We asked Allan Taylor, CEO of the Royal Bank of Canada, what he would say to people who are coming along. He said:

> I guess one of the things would be to go for it, reach out and go for the opportunities that are there. Don't just manage what is there in front of you, but also realize that you should be trying to get the maximum out of it. Do the very best that you possibly can. It's not enough just to do it and get by. What you should be thinking is, "How can I really make the very best of this?"

The successful are willing to do the menial jobs on the way up, and to do them well even if it means they have to sacrifice. In this way, they demonstrate the ability to work with and be part of a team. A record of real accomplishment and contribution at all levels, together with a willingness to rise to all, even unrealistic, demands of the job marks the career of the effective executive. Many of the CEOs we interviewed thought the way to get ahead was to contribute something extra at whatever job one holds.

André Charron of Lévesque, Beaubien sees this as a way of life:

> It's not a question of working from nine to five. I don't believe in that at all. I think a person, for the first twenty years of their working lives, should be available twenty-four hours a day, seven days a week, all year round. I don't appreciate a person who says "I can't do something because it comes up during my holidays." To me that immediately is a weakness. I think a person should stay, unless he has a commitment to his family, but ordinarily that's not my problem, it's his problem. When we ask somebody to do a job, we want *him* to do the job, not somebody else.

Understanding Of The Essentials Of The Business Or Industry
All business have their own specific challenges. To be an effective CEO, one needs to understand the key elements that make for success. More than one business has gone under due to management concentrating on volume of sales and forgetting to watch the profits. Listen to the late Val Stock of Canada Packers:

> You've got to concentrate on the key areas that affect the business, and they vary. With some it is production and for others it is sales. For some it might be research and development or cost controls. In the meat business you have to have your costs under very strict control. You've got to have the lowest cost operation and you've got to buy your raw material well. You work with very little margin so you have to control it and the expenses very carefully.

Dedication
Not all executives work long hours, but most do. It is tempting to say that those who put in extra time are workaholics (especially if one is inclined to prefer an easy pace), but most aren't, at least, not in the sense that they are driven by anxiety or fear, or work rather than going home. Most executives think their work is fun, and are motivated by the satisfaction of doing their job well rather than by the material rewards it provides. Steven Wilgar, former CEO of Warner-Lambert, recalled the excitement he felt when he changed jobs. "Talk about culture shock! It was quite a revelation. It was fun. It was a learning experience." Ross Johnson, president and CEO of RJR Nabisco, told us he also believes work has to be fun:

> Each day is for enjoyment and for living and for making yourself feel good that you're improving. If you hate accounting, or you hate some of these other things, why put yourself through it? It's torture. You've got to do what you like doing at the moment. And that may change. It doesn't mean that it won't change. A man's capable of doing many things.

Surveys of hours worked by CEOs nearly always reflect the fact that the person at the top puts in the longest hours. The CEO's job tends to be full-time, and the boundaries between work and socialization blur as CEOs keep up with the demands of their community, with their need to keep up with developments that affect the company, and the necessity of making industry contacts. All these take time and impinge on the hours available for personal concerns. As one CEO said, "What personal life?"

Robert Hurlbut, chairman and former CEO of General Foods, commented on dedication at General Foods.

> I'm not bright enough or don't have the capability to do all the things you have to do from nine to five. I don't think many people are. Our real performers here work hard. I think most people do, particularly as they are starting their careers. I don't think anyone would say that General Foods is heavily demanding of its people in terms of the hours they are required to put in to succeed. But I think those who are going to succeed do it voluntarily. Right now, we have new people in some key jobs, and those guys are just working right around the clock. One is in his mid-thirties and the other is forty-two and they are putting in incredible hours. No one is telling them to do it; they do it because they know they have a job to do.

In discussing what he looks for in new people, Laurent Beaudoin, CEO of Bombardier, said:

> To me you want someone who does not have a problem about working hard. Nothing comes easily and I like people who get involved and keep at things, who don't give up. I think today university degrees are a must because of the complexity of the operation, but you want people who really get involved, work hard and use their own judgment, not simply relying on what they learned at school and trying to apply formulas. You have to learn through hard work.

Integrity

Most of the CEOs we interviewed spoke of honesty or integrity as a very key factor they looked for in executives.

Integrity is demonstrated by treating people fairly, being straightforward rather than devious and acting in accordance with corporate policy and values and within the law. Intellectual honesty, facing reality rather than trying to fool oneself or others, was also frequently mentioned. David McCamus, president and CEO of Xerox Canada, said: "Integrity goes beyond taking money when you shouldn't. I'm talking about intellectual integrity. People who are truly honest in the sense of intellectual honesty."

A comment by William Blundell, CEO of Canadian General Electric, reflects one aspect of integrity.

> Some times you get asked to make concessions, perhaps to move someone because of a personal relationship. My own feeling on it is that you get lost if you start to make those sorts of concessions. If you do it once then you're expected to do it again. I won't say I'm uncompromising, because compromise is the name of the game in a big company.

Stamina And Health

Most executives are blessed with energy and robust physical health. This was true even before the current health and fitness fad. They have the capacity—as well as the willingness—to put in long hours and to withstand the stress that is an integral part of management. Executives must, in effect, predict the future when they make decisions, and the pressure of making major decisions can be great. Gordon Farquhar, chairman and former CEO of Aetna Canada, told us:

> Rather than what people describe as ambition, drive or whatever, I look for energy. Is the guy energetic? Does he really throw himself into the task at hand? Does he tackle it? Is he willing to stay with it or does he brush it off on somebody else? Is he willing to come forward with "effective recommendations," or does he just want somebody to tell him what to do?

Ability To Make Others Comfortable

Comfort may seem like an odd word to use, but the concept is very important in business and in life generally.

Those who lack the ability to make others comfortable fail to recognize the importance of mutual acceptance in all human relationships. They often think that creating calm and trust is someone else's responsibility. If one lacks the ability to make a superior comfortable, one reduces one's opportunities for success. People may think that doing a good job is sufficient and it is the responsibility of others to recognize their work. They think any effort on their part to be approachable is being political. On the other hand, those who are obviously ambitious and more interested in the next promotion than in doing the job well will not make others comfortable either.

Donald McIvor, former chairman and CEO of Imperial Oil, commented on the importance of interpersonal skills for success:

> I have watched quite a number of people who have had, in my view, everything it takes except interpersonal skills and therefore the ability to lead people. I have seen quite a few. Development of those interpersonal skills, I think, is something a lot of people who consider themselves CEO candidates haven't thought enough about. They haven't built their own skills. I know that people can build those skills. I don't think they're innate. I have built them largely by noticing the errors of others.

The Flip Side
On the flip side, there are some characteristics that lead to the downfall of otherwise well-qualified people. These are matters of attitude and strategy rather than of ability:

Laziness
Since lazy people usually don't want to be found out, they are often cunning and dangerous. They can become destructive when they try to protect themselves by diminishing others.

Concentration On Appearance Rather Than Substance
Some individuals have been able to gain success in school and their early careers because of their interpersonal skills

and ability to create a good impression. This strategy begins to fail when their actual performance on the job can be identified.

Extreme Ambition

The extremely ambitious are also often very able. By concentrating on their own career advancement and on short-term results they can have an advantage over those who are just trying to do a good job. But they also often try to demean their peers. One well known American executive who had rapid career advancement is reputed to have refined the technique of leaving other executives "with shit on their shoes," thus causing career problems for them and ensuring that they would not be able to challenge him for a while.

William Richards, formerly of Dome Petroleum, comments on another problem caused by the overly ambitious:

> The guy who sets out to be president distorts all of the decisions that he makes. In other words, he may be saying, "Well, this is the decision I want to make, but that's going to help me in achieving my goal of becoming president of this company, and not necessarily the best thing that ought to be done for the company." I think it's probably an unhealthy attitude.

Concentrating On Process Rather Than Results

It is more important to do the right thing than to do things right.

Fear Of Selling

Some executives are unable or unwilling to actively sell their ideas and their leadership. They fail to get the commitment of their organizations.

Forgetting Who Is The Boss

Every CEO has to report to a board of directors, but sometimes they forget who owns and controls the company and feel that they can make all the decisions. Occasionally even weak boards will rebel.

Arrogance

A CEO can easily become isolated from what is going on in his company, particularly if those who report to him do not challenge him or report the actual facts to him. This situation can encourage a CEO to feel he is omnipotent and to confuse what is good for him with what is good for the company.

Inability To Cope With The Isolation Of The Position

The almost universal complaint of CEOs concerns the loneliness of the job, and the distance that grows between them and former peers.

Failure To Staff Effectively

Some individuals try to make their position secure by ensuring that there is no one who can challenge them. They tend to hire relatively weak people who will consequently not give top performance.

Picking the winners is both difficult and uncertain for both the board and the CEO. But the choices are most critical to the future of the company. This is particularly the case when picking the top executive team. In the end it is usually the CEO who is left with that responsibility. He will be judged on his choice long after he leaves the job. It is, after all, his legacy to the company.

C H A P T E R

12

STRATEGIC
THINKING
AND PLANNING

S trategy is doing the right things. The objective of strategy
is to maximize your competitive advantage—to do better
than others who enter the same competitive arena.

There are many theories to explain why companies fail.
One of the most common causes cited by CEOs, and confirmed by our own consulting experience, is the lack of
strategic thinking and planning at the top. Warren Bennis,
the noted American academic and author, wrote:

> Most organizations reflect the uneasiness of transition for
> they were built upon certain assumptions about man and
> his environment. The environment was thought to be
> placid, predictable and uncomplicated. Organizations
> based on these assumptions will fail, if not today, then
> tomorrow. They will fail for the very same reasons that
> dinosaurs failed. The environment changes suddenly at the
> peak of their success.

John F. Fraser, CEO of Federal Industries, explained this
failure to adapt to change.

You simply can't be a CEO today and say, "I know my business and I have worked my way up through this company
and I will run it the way it has always been run. As long as
I work hard and keep my people working hard, everything
is going to be fine." No way. There are companies today,
ones that have been running for twenty-five to thirty years,
that are slowly being demolished and the management is
sitting there not even aware of what is happening. They
haven't got the strategic tools to manage their business.

Bernard Ghert of Cadillac Fairview posed a question asked
by many CEOs:

I sometimes think about change. I see the environment
changing and I wonder whether I'm adapting: in other
words, whether my management adapts so that we'll be
successful in the changing environment?

Adaptation and flexibility are key attributes in strategic
thinking and planning. Effective CEOs realize that planning
strategically is not an exact science, but rather a management process, which must be continuously adapted to the
changing business environment. This is almost impossible
in those organizations where strategic planning has become too routine and confused with operational planning.
In some companies strategic planning has become too
bureaucratic, and executives adhere too strictly to specific
methodologies.

Chief executives in North America have been utilizing various forms of strategic planning for decades. Strategic planning is, in simple terms, the process of assessing goals and
objectives effectively, then efficiently allocating resources.

Formal business planning originated in the 1950s.
During those postwar years, business was relatively
straightforward and predictable, and thus business planning for the CEO was a process that revolved around the
task of meeting customer demand. If you had a depen-
dable source of raw material, technical expertise and
marketing strength, profits followed.

Planning and decision-making were based almost entirely on financial considerations. In the 1950s the motto

was, "We want more and can get more!" And get more they did. There was a boom in key North American industries like the auto industry, the construction industry and the natural-resources industry. Full employment and ready cash for investment fed the consumer economy. Little attention was paid to emerging sociocultural and political trends.

Then, in the 1960 s competitive pressure grew from new enterprises and from western Europe, England and Japan, which recovered economically from World War Two and re-entered the world market. With this new competitive atmosphere came a growing sociocultural awareness as corporations began to realize they were simply one organization within a complex social and cultural environment. To gain a better understanding of just what was happening, some companies began to incorporate social scenarios into their planning; others turned to the emerging think-tank organizations like Herman Kahn's Hudson Institute or the Rand Corporation; and others began to realize the importance of the computer for compiling information and aiding in forecasting.

By the early 1970s strategic planning began to attract special attention as leading business schools and consulting firms developed and helped implement new planning theories and techniques. In tandem with those theories came the increasing eminence of the "corporate strategic planner" as a new member of the management team in large public companies.

But by the mid-seventies the times of assured growth and relative stability had passed. Rising energy prices, inflation, increased government intervention, growing unemployment, concern with pollution of the environment and the technological explosion—all have surfaced in the past ten years and all have had a profound effect on industry. "Discontinuity" became the new management buzz word and executives began to realize that their companies no longer had a free ride and sales and profits would no longer come easily. The credibility of strategic planning as a precise tool came under attack. Its critics argued that it was oriented toward growth in a growing market environment; that it put too much emphasis on market share and not enough emphasis on productive performances, and that it was too narrowly focused, too caught up in methodology. Planning was in the hands of staff specialists who were remote from operational management and consumers, and planning systems therefore often missed the importance of developing strategies to implement plans.

Rad Latimer, ex CEO of TransCanada Pipelines, made this point:

> It will be increasingly required that the CEO be a strategist and not just develop it as a sideline after he becomes CEO. Every time you see a vice president of planning or a vice president of strategic development, you can almost bet that nothing is ever done along that line. You know, it's a nice staff position, usually created because there's a tremendous feeling that there should be strategic development, but it isn't to the taste of the CEO who has come up all his life running operations, and so he gets the specialist to do it.

In the 1980s, as CEOs compete in an environment of limited growth potential, the mood has become more cautious and can be summed up as, "Let's hold on to what we've got." This attitude is manifested in a new business spirit characterized by a realistic attitude (no company can have, do, or be everything), a commitment to cost effectiveness, a return to basics and a more competitive, pragmatic attitude, or a will to win.

Raymond Cyr, reflecting on his time as CEO of Bell Canada, said:

> To me, the essence of the job is to recognize the nature of the corporation: what makes it tick. In Bell we had to recognize the fact that we would have competition in the terminal business. We had to ask ourselves what people buy from Bell. We don't sell a better PBX; actually we have a more limited range of things to sell. We said it is the reliability of service, so we established an advertising program where we tell the customer that we are not a cheap company and you can't buy anything from us that you can't buy more cheaply from a competitor, but when

you call us Sunday night with a problem, we will be out there to fix it, and in many cases we have systems that will tell us you have a problem before you know it. That's our strength. Part of my job has been to adjust to the period of competition and to change the culture of what we had been doing as a monopoly for a hundred years.

Organizational leaders are searching for better marketing strategies, improved techniques for cost control, better qualified personnel, new technologies and improved ways of organizing. Gerald Hobbs, formerly of Cominco, expressed it this way:

> Canada, like all North America, has had a free ride for about twenty-five years. While the rest of the world wanted our products, we didn't notice that Brazil, Korea, Japan, Taiwan and Europe were becoming extremely competitive. We accepted the loss of, say, consumer electronics and later cars to Japan and then Taiwan. We paid no attention to the fact we were becoming less and less competive in an increasingly competitive world. And when the bubble burst, as it did in the seventies, we got into the deflationary period we're now in, particularly for primary products. The chief executive officers suddenly discovered what the hell the job of CEO was—to make money for his shareholders. Quite a few companies hadn't. Some CEOs were replaced, others had to roll up their sleeves, cut the bureaucracies, sometimes by about half, and look at their costs in the light of the real world. Now, by and large, they're working CEOs, rather than presiding CEOs.

Now CEOs are reasserting their authority over all strategic planning activities. Robert DeMone, formerly CEO of Maple Leaf Mills, now CEO of Canadian Pacific Hotels Limited, is an example.

> I spend probably fifty percent of my hours on corporate development and strategy. We are looking at divesting and investing on an ongoing basis, monitoring the environment internally and externally, and easily fifty percent of my energy is devoted to that. The other fifty percent is devoted to facilitating the optimization of effort by the people who report to me.

Many CEOs have reduced the number of employees in corporate head offices so that a smaller complement of top people is taking responsibility for the strategic management of the company, and leaving operational management to subsidiary units. Other companies are striving to separate operational and budget issues from strategy, so that ideas rather than numbers dominate strategies.

There are numerous techniques for strategic planning, but what distinguishes the better ones is that they require top management to analyze the forces driving competition within their industry.

An example of such a force is that of data-processing technology in the financial services industry. Life insurance companies are required to process massive amounts of information; investment houses must account for thousands of daily transactions; banks must maintain on-line data network facilities linking hundreds of branches. A breakthrough in computer technology can therefore give a corporation an immediate, vital advantage over its competition is each of these sectors. In this sense, the better plans are more pragmatic and more in keeping with the real issues that must be addressed by CEOs today.

Let's look further at Canadian financial institutions and how they carry out their strategic planning. In the fifties and sixties, banks took deposits and gave loans; life insurers sold whole life, some term and even a few annuities; trust companies were very much fiduciary by nature. There was a comfortable market niche for everyone and regulations defined the ball park where you played. Beginning in the seventies and continuing to the present there has been a shift from a few products and services to an explosion into a multiplicity of offerings. Banking alone has gone from a three-course meal to buffet brunch. Clean lines of product separation have become diffused. Deregulation is a fact in the United States, as it is in Great Britain and certainly all signs suggest it will occur in Canada.

All this means that, among financial institutions, there is fiercer competition, tightened margins, rapidly evolving technology and shifting regulations.

All the chief executive officers of financial institutions with whom we met recognize that their organizations need to be market, customer and product-driven. They realize that productivity is a key to profitability and that management will need to continue to introduce new competitive products and services domestically and internationally, even as they stay abreast of changes in regulations.

The challenge will be to adjust to the new world in spite of the long and, in some cases, restraining traditions. And that is where serious strategic planning has to begin. Rowland Frazee, the well-known and respected former CEO of the Royal Bank of Canada, gave this view on the need for strategic thinking and planning at the CEO's level.

> There are many [CEOs] who believe in strategic planning but those who don't will have to. Chief executives are going to have to establish some sort of image or mission or direction for their organizations. The days of just taking advantage of opportunities as they come along are gone.

So where does one begin?

Once financial services could be visualized as a spectrum that moved from simple advice to consumers to complex, highly individualized advice; and a second spectrum that moved from a simple standard mass product to a highly customized one. Traditionally, banks, life insurance companies and credit unions sat at one end of the spectrum, providing simple advice and standard mass-market products. Tax advisors and investment counselors represented the other end, giving highly customized advice and tailored individual products. In the middle were investment planners, insurance planners, mutual funds and the like.

But recently lines have become blurred, with some interesting results. Trust companies are now extremely diversified: at one end they offer highly customized fiduciary advice, and at the other end, mass simple products such as deposit-taking and consumer lending. Banks have pushed out from the traditional mode and now offer RRSPs, discount brokerage services and the like. And large investment houses have moved into forms of banking with cash-management accounts.

A key priority for effective strategic thinking in financial institutions involves sorting through where they are on this spectrum and understanding where they should be. In short, what their market niches are. Richard Thomson recollected a talk he gave to business students at the University of Western Ontario:

> I said the most difficult question is, "Where do you want to go? I mean where do you want the institution to go?" And the other difficult question is, "Once you decide where you want the institution to go, how do you get it there?" Because you don't have any levers or buttons or orders that you can issue. You've got to find a way to get there without issuing too many orders. So you've got to know an awful lot about your business, your competitor's business—and you've got to define your business broadly, because it takes a lot of that kind of knowledge to know where you want to go. Everybody will tell you where you should go, but you have to decide.

Recognizing the public's new financial needs and identifying the consumers' needs at specific times in their lives is fundamental to good strategic thinking. It is part of the reason for the proliferation of new financial products and instruments we see being offered by financial institutions across the market, products that are more often than not customized to various age ranges, to income levels, to marital status and so on. This is also the case with many other industries, leading ultimately to a drive for more innovative, higher quality products and services.

Finance is, of course, only one industry. What of the others?

Our own experience coupled with our discussions with chief executive officers leads us to conclude that there are some sound fundamentals being followed by CEOs who believe in sound strategic thinking and planning. They recognize that there can be no one best strategic planning system. Rather, the system must fit its unique organizational culture. For example, a service business cannot easily adopt generic strategies and techniques that, for the most part, have been formed to fit the manufacturing sector. As John Fraser has said: "You can't be a great strategic thinker unless you have a pretty good knowledge of the industry you are in."

Chief executives ensure that strategic planning is not isolated as a function. But rather, it is an integral part of, and support to, the strategic management thrust. Many corporations in Canada have been too slow in recognizing that strategic management must integrate all the parts of the corporate system: strategy, capital, people, rewards, marketing systems and so on into a coherent whole.

Successful top management keeps this strategic planning process from becoming too prescriptive. They let it be flexible so that it can stimulate creativity and innovation, which are essential if the organization intends to develop new products and services, new marketing and new means of distribution.

Today's leaders know that sociocultural trends and issues are central to strategic planning, rather than peripheral. Investment in research is necessary to ensure that corporate strategies are consistent with considerations that influence government policies. Only through this environmental scanning can institutions identify their opportunities and risks.

Peter Gordon was still CEO of Stelco when we talked with him. He emphasized this broadening horizon of strategic thinking.

> John [John Allen, who is now CEO of Stelco] and I spend more time worrying about things that are extraneous to our ability to make and sell steel. We're worried about government regulations; we're worried about changes in markets; we're worried about protectionism in the United States; we're worried about environmental regulations; we're worried about takeovers—that wasn't a problem twenty-five years ago; we're worried about our relationship with our people.

Traditionally, too many company information systems have lacked information on product profitability. Better methods of defining and allocating the costs of various products and services are needed to provide a future base for determining sound cost or value-based pricing strategies.

Organizational leaders also insist that strategic planning approaches incorporate customer and competitor analysis and create products and services needed by consumers. Customers are increasingly sophisticated and selective about products and services. These changes, plus intense competition, make such analysis essential. However, principal strategy should not be only market-driven. New ideas should not come only from customers. More companies, particularly consumer ones, need to emphasize service.

Effective CEOs are committed to driving strategic planning downward into their organizations by incorporating ideas from people who are on the firing line, meeting customers and the competition. Strategy must be "owned" by the people who make things happen in their organization. This occurs only if there is respect for their experience, judgement and pragmatism.

Allan Marchment, CEO of Guaranty Trust, explained the process.

> My job is to look at the total picture and see that the growth rates are satisfactory, because we're compared with other companies, and we know we've got to grow faster than others because we're coming from further behind. But once that's decided, the strategies and the implementation for the various parts of the organization are put together by the people responsible for them. With a few exceptions, they are free to pick their priorities.

Dean Muncaster, former CEO of Canadian Tire, added,

> Yes, when you talk about strategy and planning activities they must be done in the line functions—the people who are going to have to make it work are the ones who are developing the plan.

Raymond Cyr commented on keeping strategy development within the company when he was CEO of Bell Canada:

As far as strategic planning is concerned, we have had outsiders come in to work with us on retreats and so forth, but
it has never worked for us. I think it is difficult for anyone
to understand a regulated industry unless they come from
one. We aren't free to make the economic decisions we
would like because we are regulated by the CRTC. We make
a lot of investments that aren't profitable because they are
part of our charter obligations.

Another factor that major corporations include in their
strategic planning is the internationalization of business
and, with it, real global competition. Foreign competition
has meant that their company's position in the market has
become the key priority in the minds of CEOs, because
maintaining it has often become synonymous with corporate survival.

Allan Taylor, CEO of the Royal Bank of Canada, said:

I think we do the country a great disservice if we don't realize that we need bigger and stronger financial institutions,
not a lot more smaller ones, if we are to compete internationally. Internationalization of the [commercial] marketplace and of the financial marketplace is a fact of life. We
have banks that can stand up to the best; and if it isn't
going to happen with us it isn't going to happen with
anybody. So we just have to do it. You are going to hear us
speak up very often and frequently about the need to ex-
pand services generally so we become larger and therefore
stronger financial institutions in order to be internationally
competitive.

To sum up, the CEO must learn to distinguish the following:

- Strategic planning, which is concerned with determining
  the direction in which the enterprise should be going.
- Action planning, which sets out how each existing business unit within the enterprise will achieve the goals and
  objectives within the defined direction.
- Business development, which focuses on developing
  new products and services, joint ventures and acquisitions beyond the traditional base of the institution.

The key to growth and profit lies in superior execution based on the fast-thinking, action-oriented strategies. Successful CEOs must therefore be, above all, flexible. They must have good natural instincts so they can quickly adapt their planning to new situations. They hope in this way to avoid the fate of the dinosaur.

13

REVIVING THE ENTREPRENEURIAL SPIRIT

John Fraser discussed what he looks for in a manager.

> We look for entrepreneurial skills and we look at the type of work they have done. Have they clearly indicated they really like business? One kid we interviewed ran a rug-cleaning business. He got a rug cleaner, then he got a panel truck and put his name on it. He made all kinds of money and put himself through school. That's the kind of person we are looking for. Don't give me those MBAs who came out of the anthropology school. We need people who are really interested in business: we need people who understand how the various pieces fit together to make money. Do you realize how few people know how to make money? Too many young people don't know what making money is. They think it's something that happens by government decree.

Sadly, this lack of entrepreneurship is in part a direct result of the overly structured climate within large corporations.

As they grow, many companies move from risk-taking and innovation to bureaucracy and risk avoidance.

Successful companies always have a competitive edge. It can be in the form of a superior product, or a more efficient cost-effective manufacturing process, or better sales and distribution methods, or more innovative research and development. Having such a competitive edge gives the company a better ability to compete at a given time.

Too often, large mature corporations lose their competitive edge and, therefore, their ability to keep up at a time when the rate of change is accelerating. To ensure that innovation and creativity do not lose out to rigidity and conservatism, the CEO needs to sustain an entrepreneurial spirit. For this task he needs to be, in part, an entrepreneur himself.

Most of us associate the entrepreneur with the man or woman who starts a business and who brings to it a flair for innovation, a daring spirit and tremendous energy. Usually entrepreneurial enterprises are not large, certainly not when compared to the major public corporations over which the chief executive officers we have been discussing preside.

Entrepreneurial ventures are usually controlled and run by highly creative, very independent people who are willing to risk a great deal for even greater possible return. Interestingly, it is the one area of business where female role models are most abundant. Most companies run by women were started by women entrepreneurs. In recent years, women have made great inroads in small business, and that requires a high degree of entrepreneurial spirit. But women entrepreneurs are not new. Certainly Mary Kay took some of her cues from Helena Rubenstein. The fashion and food industries have also attracted both male and female entrepreneurs—as have many expanding areas, like the new fitness industry. When women have been able to obtain financial backing, they have proved themselves capable of founding and operating large, innovative companies. As these companies merge with older companies, a new pool of female talent is being created.

The bywords of the entrepreneur are risk for creativity, fun and profit. This is a far different philosophy from that found in large public companies whose very well-being is often seen to be based on avoiding innovation and independence; steady annual gains are more the norm than a spectacular return from a high-risk new venture.

Indeed, it seems to be almost an inevitable part of the life cycle of an organization that in time it will lose the entrepreneurial nature that it once possessed. Too often companies follow a life cycle that starts in the "embryonic business" phase, followed by the "entrepreneurial" stage, which ultimately brings the organization (assuming it survives) to the "mature corporate growth" stage. That sometimes leads to the "aging company" stage and, unfortunately, to the "troubled company and bankruptcy" stage. Let's look more carefully at the first three, in the hopes of avoiding the last two.

In the embryonic stage the environment is typified by just two words: high uncertainty. The creator of the enterprise is a risk-taker, and if he or she is successful, this stage is often characterized by rapid sales growth, high need for cash and a very competitive environment. Sometimes, however, in this embryonic stage the venture is barely profitable.

Whatever the profits, the chief executive is typically the owner who runs a one-man show. The company closely reflects its leader's personality if for no other reason than he or she has invested everything to finance the venture. Its survival will rest on this individual's energy, motivation, decision-making and willingness to take risk. It is a hands-on job and it is all-consuming.

If the venture is fortunate, it will gradually move to stage two, entrepreneurial growth. By this time it will be a private company, or it may even have blossomed into a small public entity. Typically it experiences slower growth but higher volume of sales. Expansion and demand have increased the company's need for capital. Certainly, the company is better balanced and more established, and its profitability, while perhaps low, at least exists.

Later it begins to need certain support systems—better information, more control over inventories, accounts receivable systems, operating procedures and so on. Data-processing systems look attractive. Someone starts talking about something called strategic planning. The time for professional management has arrived, and a means for better organization for future growth must be found.

It's at this critical stage that the owner-manager, with his or her hands-on style, can no longer manage it all. It has reached the professional management stage, in which it needs the more specialized skills of others to complement the owner's innovation and creativity. Yet it is still a growing entity, probably still in one line of business and still vulnerable. It needs stability, but it also requires new capital through refinancing, joint venture, even merger or, perhaps, a public stock offering. There is still great risk and the continuing need for the entrepreneur's creative energy. He or she remains the chief executive officer, the chairman of the board and, if not the sole majority owner, the major shareholder. Even though the owner may have a larger management team, it is still his or her game to win or lose.

The story of Noma Industries in many ways parallels these stages. It was started in 1950 as a small private company by two newly arrived immigrants, Theresa Beck and her son Henry Thomas Beck. They purchased a small electric-component assembly business. Mrs. Beck took responsibility for the administration and assembly, and her son, a graduate engineer from London University, quickly learned the art of selling.

Through sheer hard work and concentration on the matters at hand the company grew. By 1963 it had achieved sufficient size to buy Noma Lights Canada Limited from its American parent company. Mrs. Beck continued to keep a strong hand on finance and administration, her son Tom on marketing and sales. Rudolph Koehler, who had joined the Becks in 1956, watched over manufacturing. The three met daily in the plant for lunch, which was usually prepared by Mrs. Beck.

By 1964 they had begun to hire outside management, and the era of professional management had begun. By

1972 revenues had grown to $13 million, and the Becks were ready to go public. They did so that year, listing and trading shares on the Toronto stock market. This gave the company access to investment capital to finance its next stage of growth, and it also created the opportunity for its employees to participate in share ownership.

Today, consolidated sales of the Noma group of companies exceed $500 million. There are twenty-one operating plants in Canada and the U.S. Noma's markets are international. Its electrical and mechanical products serve both industrial and consumer markets.

Noma is moving into the corporate growth stage. Both Thomas Beck and Rudolph Koehler, chairman and president respectively, are aware of the critical need to sustain innovation and entrepreneurship. Noma utilizes the business-unit concept—highly autonomous profit centers, each with strong experienced management given lots of room to operate independently.

They stress quality and integrity and, as Beck said, "We pay attention to detail. That's the key to running each of the small businesses we have." He and Koehler operate from a small corporate office and rarely interfere with the units.

In explaining their management style, Beck said, "Occasionally we feel we have to make a point. First we suggest. If nothing happens, we strongly suggest; then we will urge. And if nothing still happens, then we will tell." They believe in innovation and encourage it in their business units. They believe that they can avoid the disasters that can occur when a company reaches the mature corporate growth stage by keeping it lean, by protecting the decentralized management system and by ensuring that viability and entrepreneurship are built in at each level. They encourage share ownership by management and employees. Rudolph Koehler emphasized:

> The key is to sustain an entrepreneurial business with good management skills. Mrs. Beck created an environment where it was each person's business. We need to be demanding, but sincere and caring. We need to constantly

develop our people. We must always reward and recognize
them.

The professional stage leads, in time, to a further one. The
nature of the enterprise changes and eventually it enters a
mature corporate growth stage. It may also merge with a
larger company that is already at the mature corporate
growth stage. The company is now, in all likelihood, public
and probably in more than one line of business, at least
some of which will be cash generators. Earnings are higher
and more predictable. Probably the organization suffers
from certain problems, not the least of which is uneven
management.

At this stage there is a formalized management structure. Strategic planning, while never perfect, is at least
represented by operating plans and budgets. Management
controls are in place, mostly computer-based. New
products are well researched and introduced to the market
carefully. By now the owner-manager may have given way
to a professional chief executive officer who is accountable
to a board of directors. While outside demands are increasing, this leader is also having to find ways to increase
productivity, contain rising costs and encourage better systems planning. Stability is important and is a key standard
of performance. The board, and therefore the chief executive officer, has a strong desire *not* to be surprised. Too
much innovation, independent action and risk-taking
simply are not at the top of the board's list of qualities essential in its CEO. As well, the new constituencies—the outside shareholder groups—are beginning to expect solid
growth, return on investment, earnings and dividends,
year after year.

Coping with the latter stages of the life cycle is not easy.
The watchword is caution. Employees in large corporations
often say, "You don't make mistakes and survive in our company." Indeed, it is one of the most common phrases in the
corporate business world. Generations of managers have
grown up in countless corporations throughout North
America knowing that a significant mistake could be their
one serious pitfall on the way up the corporate ladder. To

avoid it, they work hard, pay careful attention to detail, examine each issue carefully and make full use of the company's resources and its support systems. In this way, they are able to make good, if cautious, decisions.

Large corporations emphasize team spirit and the ability to get along with others. If a bright young manager suggests an innovative new idea, his boss is likely to reply, "Excellent, Bill, but why didn't you test it with John?" Or even better: "Let's put a small team together to look at all sides of the matter. If we can still be positive about it, let's then document it. In the meantime let me give some thought the best way to expose it to some folks at the next level." These delayed responses will certainly not encourage the young innovator to go off on his own to exercise his independence and creativity.

But the need to survive in an increasingly competitive and uncertain marketplace has thrown some of this traditional caution to the winds. Richard Thomson of the Toronto Dominion Bank reflected:

> It's so easy in an organization not to take risks. You've got to fight bureaucracy all the time because so many people are content to retire halfway along the path, and that can happen regardless of position. I'm sure every organization has people like this. They aren't about to take any risk and they aren't about to change anything they don't have to change. But the market will force them to change.

In recent years, many have asked how a large corporation, slowed down by its lack of competitiveness in product and service, can recreate some of the entrepreneurial spirit of its early days. Charles Hantho, the solid and determined CEO of the chemical giant, C-I-L said:

> I think the challenges are really challenges of managing in mature markets. Even when you have a good defensible, viable business, the challenge is to keep throwing in new ideas and doing things differently and beating out competition. In a mature business, this is the kind of a challenge that people have a hard time viewing positively.

Some CEOs have established special-project teams or task forces, which bring together bright, talented people from various parts of the organization and put them to work on a particular innovative task. They do not usually deal with high-risk issues, nor is there any pressure placed on them to deliver a large return to the company in terms of dollars. But freed from the stultification of day-to-day systems, such "think teams" are controllable, educational and often beneficial to those who participate. But they alone are not the answer; rather these one-time attempts at freedom from the bureaucracy of the corporation are little more than token entrepreneurism.

There are occasions when task forces work and return large dollars. A major Canadian manufacturing corporation concerned about its rising costs and poor productivity finally decided to establish an internal task force to come up with creative ways to eliminate unnecessary costs. It wisely chose its brightest and fastest-rising stars, men and women from each function, and added a few wise and older veterans to the mixture. The CEO gave this ten-member group total freedom. They could talk to anyone they wanted, have access to whatever data they needed and even hire their choice of an outside consultant—providing the latter acted only as a facilitator to the task force.

The team attacked its mission with enthusiasm and dedication. Within three months it had fifty specific recommendations, which, when implemented, reduced costs by millions of dollars.

Other corporations have created separate organizational units—departments, even divisions—to try to start up a new entrepreneurial effort, completely divorced from the parent. But these have not recaptured the lost spirit of enterprise—the willingness to take the risks, the innovativeness and the creativity—within the corporation itself.

Yet innovation isn't mysterious, nor is it confined to a special species of human being. What is needed is purposeful pursuit of innovation. In fact, any organization can be entrepreneurial. Some observers, including Peter Drucker, believe that it is not in the small enterprise where one finds serious innovation, but in big companies and institutions. Smaller companies simply cannot afford the costs of or the time for productive innovations. In fact, many successful innovators are found in large organizations. They have five to eight years of experience; they can learn; they can get the tools; they know what cash flow is, and what rate of return is; they understand teamwork and they know how to delegate. This discipline, these tools and this knowledge are not found in abundance in small businesses.

And there is no question that some major corporations are more innovative, more creative and, as a result, more competitive and aggressive in the marketplace. Somehow, they have harnessed a spirit of creativity and risk-taking that attracts and retains outstanding talent.

How do they do it?

Our experience and observation lead us to conclude that it comes down to this simple question: does the chief executive officer really want to see more innovation, more creativity, a more aggressive approach to the marketplace? Is he prepared to let people make mistakes—even big ones? Most organizational leaders will start out by answering yes to these questions, but they modify their response after probing. Many will become somewhat cautious and, by their caution, begin to reflect the true nature of their corporation—safe, staid and committed to meeting the expectation of their conservative investors. As one CEO stated:

> I've always believed that some people can't work in a large corporation. Once you get to the top you don't have any constraints. But while working your way up you must remember that there's the rule book, the unwritten rules. There are the things you do and you cannot do, and you can either thrive under those conditions or you can flounder. Some people work better outside the system, like the real entrepreneurs that we are all familiar with. It's a damn good thing for our country that there are people who thrive under those circumstances.

But other CEOs are genuinely enthusiastic about what their organizations are doing. These CEOs encourage their people to attempt to perform their jobs in a better way, even to challenge whether their job is worth doing in the first place—and that is taking real risk. A leading Canadian financial institution tackled its growing overhead costs by encouraging a productivity-improvement program. All its management and supervisory employees were asked to review their own jobs in this way. Those who did courageously suggest that their particular positions could be redundant were reassigned temporarily to a "management bank" until a permanent reassignment could be made.

These CEOs also encourage their people to examine their markets at home and abroad to find out if someone somewhere has a better idea or product or innovation. And if something is found, then the CEOs make the resources available to incorporate it into their own environment. The Japanese have set the model for finding new product innovations in other markets. They have skillfully adapted these products (televisions, microchips, automobiles or whatever), improved on them and sold them back into the markets that the product came from.

These CEOs encourage their people to be aware of changing conditions—demographics, attitudes, motivations, habits. In order to do this, management has to be "on the ground"—close to their customers, where the whole demand for newer and better begins. The major breweries have for years stayed close to the consumer since they must fight for every precious share of the market with constant advertising and special promotions.

The CEOs who encourage the spirit of entrepreneurship let their employees know they are serious by providing the right tools—access to good library and research facilities, funds for further study and education. And they don't turn the tap on or off every time results lag.

Bell-Northern Research is just one outstanding example of real commitment to innovative research. They train their employees to understand the importance of return on investments, cost-benefit analysis and bottom-line performance as part of the reporting requirements on new proposals. This training encourages a business-oriented assessment at all times by those who are doing the creative thinking. Such business discipline helps them avoid having too many proposals turned down.

No matter how small the achievement, these CEOs give recognition by personally acknowledging excellence in innovation and by letting people know they have been seen to do their job well. They force their compensation and reward systems to give proper weight to innovation, creativity and excellence by building these qualities into the performance-review systems.

Above all, these organizational leaders simply allow most of this to take place. They themselves do not need to be demonstrable entrepreneurs. But they must build a climate for innovation into their corporations and serve as an example of those who have been able to combine both managerial and entrepreneurial talents. David McCamus described his job this way:

> You have to behave like an entrepreneur. You can't run a company with one entrepreneur and one hundred thousand bureaucrats. You can't be the only entrepreneur, so you must learn how to show entrepreneurship.

The successful entrepreneur is the one who has learned some of the important elements of managing, and the successful chief executive officer is the one who has room for some entrepreneurship in his style. Without it, he will become the cautious guardian of the status quo and his organization will be innovative only in the art of risk avoidance.

CHAPTER

14

WOMEN
EXECUTIVES

M adame President is a term not often heard in the corridors of executive power. When it is heard, it usually refers to the founder or inheritor of the company. There are some very prominent and very successful women CEOs in Canada, but they all have a very strong or controlling equity in the companies they manage.

We failed to find any women who are the chief executive officers of major Canadian publicly held corporations. (However, we did meet with Angela Cantwell Peters, who retired as CEO of Bowring Brothers Limited.) The fact that women have not yet reached the position of CEO is not surprising given that CEOs attain their position in their late forties or fifties—after careers that may have spanned twenty-five years. Yet twenty-five years ago very few women entered business in occupations or functions that led to the top job. Typically, the women who are upwardly mobile in corporations have tended to be in specialist roles, such as advertising, promotion or accounting functions, rather than in the main-line functions of business—marketing service, production or finance.

We think that this absence of female CEOs of major public companies will not continue for more than five or, at the very most, ten years. One has only to read the appointment notices in the papers to be impressed with the increasing number of women who are reaching the vice presidential level. Such announcements are beginning to reflect the move of women into the critical operational areas of major corporations.

During our consulting careers and more recently as part of the research for this book, we have spoken with many women in executive ranks to learn what their experiences have been and what their attitudes are. These women in the next few years will likely begin to occupy the CEO's chair. They are on the leading edge of advancement because they occupy the most senior positions ever held in their companies by women. They are generally in their late thirties and early forties. There are some important differences between these women's backgrounds and those of male chief executive officers, differences sufficiently marked even in our small sample that we think they are likely to be representative of the larger population of upwardly mobile women in business.

Compared to the men who have achieved the position of chief executive officer, the women, on average, come from more affluent families. In most families the father was, or still is, a professional or a manager. In most instances their mothers have not held full-time paying jobs outside the home. Most of these women come from small families and were usually the oldest, and often the only, child. Fewer of these upwardly mobile women appear to view their childhood years as being ones of great happiness. The reason for this is not clear. It may simply reflect the tendency of older people (as a group, the CEOs we talked with were older than the upwardly mobile women) to remember the good and forget the bad; it may reflect a greater awareness on the part of the women to family undercurrents; or it may reflect a true difference in family relations.

The educational backgrounds of these women are generally similar to those of male executives, with the majority having one or more university degrees or a professional designation in law or accounting. Nearly all achieved high marks at school. Many were also very active socially and had leadership roles in school and were active in sports. While women were a rarity in MBA programs thirty years ago, in the last ten years there has been a great increase in the number of women MBAs. With this background an increasing number of women will be knocking on the doors of the executive suites in years to come. The high marks in education achieved by them reflect the fact that, like the chief executive officers we met, these women were brought up in homes where hard work and good solid achievement were expected.

Women demonstrating strong upward mobility seem to show some differences in their career patterns when compared to men who have achieved senior management positions. As a group, these women have been more mobile, changing employers several times and, in almost every instance, joining their present employer in a professional or executive role. It would appear that women have to change jobs more often in order to get ahead, perhaps because their capacity for advancement has been underestimated by those who have managed them in their earlier positions.

Establishing friendly and cooperative interpersonal relationships seems to be important to women. In dealing with people in the workplace on issues that generate severe opposition or resistance to change, they are slightly less inclined than men to press the issue. Because these upwardly mobile women have a higher sense of tact and more sensitivity to the feelings of others in the organization, they have developed a somewhat greater understanding of supervisory techniques. They also demonstrate a somewhat higher need for achievement, although at the early stages of their careers this need was expressed more in terms of the specifics of their particular jobs than is the case for men, who seem to develop a stronger management orientation earlier.

Women in business adopt over time a number of tendencies associated with measures of "masculinity," a term that includes characteristics such as impatience, aggressiveness and opportunism. With respect to these characteristics businesswomen hold a position about halfway between that of the average man and that of the average woman.

Further comparisons of personality characteristics between upwardly mobile women and successful male senior executives show that these women seem to develop a similar sense of poise or ability to meet and be effective with others. They have a high level of confidence. Their levels of social maturity are about equal to those of men. They seem to be more orderly and systematic in their problem-solving and more flexible and adaptable in facing business situations.

If we compare entry-level women with men at senior levels of management, we find the average entry-level women surpassing the average top executive in speed and accuracy with detail (a skill that is greater at each successive management level). Women are more accurate in evaluating the logic of arguments. Women entering one of the business career paths that lead to the CEO position are very competitive with men. They also compare favorably with men who have attained executive levels, suggesting that women who have the opportunity and desire to reach the top will continue to be very competitive. Nevertheless, while upwardly mobile women are ambitious, they are more concerned than their male counterparts with developing a balanced life, show more concern about people and are more interested in the arts. Even so they have a slightly lower sense of control over their lives.

Because the characteristics of individuals who enter a specific business function eventually become the characteristics of those who emerge in the top jobs, it is helpful to look at the differences between male and female applicants for sales and marketing positions. These jobs in the past have been predominantly male and have clearly had the potential to lead to very senior appointments.

Upwardly mobile women at this entry level are better than the average upwardly mobile man in their ability to learn things quickly, surpassing nearly 60 percent of the men. In addition, women are much better in their speed and accuracy with detailed work, surpassing 75 percent of the men. Women are slightly less practical than the men; however, they are better at using logic and analysis to think through complex problems, showing particular strength in their ability to evaluate the validity of logical arguments. This seems to challenge the conventional wisdom that women are emotional rather than logical—at least in reference to those with high career aspirations. The women as a group do not seem to be more intellectually inclined than the men. They do show evidence of being more planned and organized in their approach to work, and of being ready to work harder than the men.

Women in sales or marketing positions seem to have a narrower range of sales interest than do the men, and they have a greater need to "believe in" the product or service. This suggests that women's sales approaches will be more personal and more service-oriented that those of men, and that once convinced of a product or service, women have greater readiness to work hard to exhibit a higher level of perseverance. As we know, women have achieved outstanding success in areas such as residential real estate. It is likely that this comes about because of their sensitivity to the feelings of others, attention to detail and perseverance.

When we have met and interviewed women at the leading edge of advancement in management, they have often impressed us as being confident, competent and largely free from the militant aspects of feminism. They want to get on with their work and not concern themselves with questions of gender. Nevertheless, it is still predominantly a male business environment, and they have had and continue to experience some gender-related problems. One woman vice president, on joining her company, was being welcomed by the president. He explained to her that it was his intention to treat her just as he treated all of the other vice presidents (who were all men). However, there was one exception, and that was when he said, "Having lunch together is simply not in the cards." His concern? Being seen with an unknown woman in a social setting. That is just one example of the fact that women are still not able to move as freely today in society as men are.

Women are often unable to deal with male habits and the communications systems of their male peers. For example, one woman asked, "When the guys begin to talk about their favourite 'jocks', what am I supposed to say? Wow, what a body?" In the informal moments before and after meetings, men are more comfortable with each other than they are with women in the business environment.

Many of the upwardly mobile women we spoke with think that men waste a lot of time on unnecessary talk, be it about last night's game or a weekend of fishing or hunting. Women would rather get on with the job at hand. Indeed, a number of women say they often get impatient with the amount of discussion among their male peers even during the course of business meetings. They get tired of talking a problem to death. As one woman executive said, "I'm amazed at the amount of time that men take to discuss a problem as they sit around a committee table." In short, these women believe that they are less political than their male counterparts and that they can be more blunt and can focus on facts more quickly.

Gender differences sometimes work to the women's advantage, however. Many women executives believe that a competent senior woman often gets more opportunities for prominence simply because of her sex. Interestingly, these women regard this as unfair and believe that it often creates resentment on the part of men. While they accept the fact that the publicity surrounding the appointments of women senior executives helps create a greater awareness of opportunities for women, as a group they do not like to be rewarded simply because they are women.

Angela Cantwell Peters, former CEO of Bowrings, commented on tokenism:

> Every now and then I get uptight because people say that the woman is a token. Fifty people will say to you, "You're a token on that board." But I say, "Don't look at me that way because I think every man there is a token as well."

He's there either because of his position or his name and so
on. I'm not saying that everyone around the table is a
token, but a lot of people are tokens.

The more senior upwardly mobile women who are already in vice presidential or equivalent positions do not
think they fit the old stereotype of being emotional and
more strongly oriented to people than to facts. They do
believe that they are more sensitive to the feelings of
others but that this sensitivity is a strength, not a weakness. Further, they do not believe that sensitivity gets in
the way of making tough decisions when they are necessary.

These women believe they are more productive on the
job. There is no doubt that one of the reasons for this is that
they need to meet other important claims on their time,
particularly from their families, thus they have no other
choice but to use their time very effectively. It is their impression that they are better than their male counterparts
at getting down to work, and are more concerned with the
process of getting things done efficiently and working the
system effectively.

The senior executive women we talked to look back and
believe that they tried to fill many roles at once, such as
manager, spouse and mother. They believe that the younger
women coming up in organizations today will be less likely
to follow this pattern and will be able to concentrate on establishing their careers, if not without marriage, at least
without children. For the most part, the women that we
talked to were brought up in homes where the spoken or un-
spoken assumption was that they would marry and have
children—the traditional feminine role. The most serious personal problems they have experienced in their rise to the near
top are the extreme pressures on their time as they have tried
to juggle two or three major roles and the guilt feelings that
arise from trying to do so. These expectations have had
another effect on them in the workplace. They simply cannot,
because of the time pressures that they face, do things on the
spur of the moment, such as going out and having a drink
with their male peers after work.

As they move through their careers and face these challenges, these women undergo a change in self-perception
that is profound and difficult. Among the most common
difficulties that we heard were the following: women must
become tempermentally more like men in order to compete in what is still a predominantly male environment;
women must overcome some of the nurturing attitudes in-
culcated by their early unbringing.

Because of this women may feel less confident than men
in business. Perhaps it is because they have not had many
opportunities to compete with men (except in the educational environment, where they do it very well). Perhaps it
is because they were brought up to expect that the male
should be superior in some way. In any event, their lack of
confidence can impair the easy and effective use of their
ability.

Upwardly mobile women who depart from the traditional roles are often apprehensive over the trade-offs.
Motherhood is demanding and so is an upwardly mobile
career, and the balance is difficult to attain. Angela
Cantwell Peters responded to the dual demands of
motherhood and executive status in this way:

> It is a tough job. It really is. It's very hard, and not only
> physically very hard—working overtime and bringing
> things home—but also the regrets. I do not regret my
> career, but I wish I'd been with my daughter more, and I
> couldn't. I really regret that.

For some the problem is resolved by the determination not
to marry, or if married, not to have children. We have seen
some rational attempts to deal with this matter of trade-
offs. The most successful method seems to have been to
hire live-in help. With or without such help, some opt for a
degree of role reversal, where the man assumes more
domestic responsibilities. We encountered one woman
who was a very effective district sales manager for a large
national company. The marital home was hers; she had a
five-year financial plan which was ahead of schedule, and
she had no plans for children. Her husband, who was interested in antique guns, had an undemanding job in an

antique shop. In cases like this, women have usually said that they were very content with the arrangement.

Nevertheless, in most instances the expectation that the husband will do better than the wife seems to run deep, and even very successful women seem to want a husband they can look up to as well as love. Perhaps for this reason they are reluctant to compete with men in traditionally male roles. The more senior women we talked to think that the younger women will likely be more able to find workable arrangements to deal with these issues.

Another difficulty that women have to contend with is that there are few role models for them; therefore, the road to the top is less clear and the decisions that must be made along the way are more complex. However, most of the women have had male mentors who have contributed greatly to their careers. They do not think that they have had fewer mentors than their male counterparts but they do feel that they have had to be a little more aggressive in seeking help.

None of the successful women interviewed thought that they have been subjected to sexual harassment on the job. They all agreed that it can be a problem for women who are in more junior and therefore less powerful positions and they believe that capable and competent women who have self-confidence can deal with these types of issues.

Women already in the executive ranks have some advice for the younger women following them up the corporate ladder. The first:
- Don't try to do everything at once by starting a career, entering marriage and becoming a mother all at the same time. Demands placed on young, well-educated men and women entering the corporate workforce are such that if one wants to succeed, all the characteristics, attitudes and strategies described in this book as important early steps in career development are doubly important for young women. Trying to meet the demands of a new marriage or young children while at the same time meeting the demands and expectations of bosses looking for high energy and dedication from their new entrants is a next to impossible task.
- Seek industries that are more receptive to women ex-

ecutives, specifically financial service and the high-tech industries. Avoid traditionally male industries, such as construction, mining and some manufacturing where there is still little if any opportunity for women to move into senior executive ranks. Pick the right industries, particularly those where the consumer of the product and/or service is represented at least as much by the female population as by the male.

The advice to young women on how to handle themselves in order to get ahead is very similar to that which is offered to young men, which can be summed up as follows: get a broad education, be professional, work extremely hard, grab opportunities and do your best. They add two important further recommendations: the first is to maintain a healthy sense of humor and the second is to try to avoid feeling guilty.

Of the many women that we talked to, only a few really believe that they have a chance to move into the chief executive officer's position. They see themselves as the vanguard, paving the way and helping to develop a greater awareness of the capabilities of women as executives in major corporations. When challenged, many of these women wondered whether, if offered the top job, they would really want it.

There is no doubt that senior executive opportunities in the corporate world, particularly in the service industries, are quickly opening up for women. There is every reason to believe that these opportunities will be filled quickly and that in the not-too-distant future we will begin to see female CEOs. However, there is yet another avenue for their talents. Many of the senior executive women we talked to forecast that many of the young women entering the corporate workforce today will eventually marry and will drop out of the corporate world during the years of child-rearing. However, they will probably return to the business world, not in major public corporations but in more entrepreneurial roles. Even today, women are involved in a high proportion of startups, and the prospect of more women with sound corporate business backgrounds doing just that in the years to come is very encouraging.

15

MEASURING
U P

America's business leaders can no longer take corporate survival for granted. "The turmoil in corporate America is forcing the nation's business leaders to undertake the most radical reassessment of their practices and beliefs since the end of World War Two," says Steven Prokesch in an article he wrote for the *New York Times* on January 25, 1987. American chief executives and their Canadian counterparts had it easy thirty years ago. The war had left the economies of Germany and Japan in ruins. Most other nations were no rival for North America. There was so much pent-up demand that major corporations had their hands full simply serving the domestic market. It was a sellers' market, and the major corporate objective was to build increased capacity—more often than not at the expense of quality. Measurement of performance was pretty fundamental—this year's sales compared to last year's. The balance sheet, return on equity and other such indicators were mostly ignored.

During the fifties and sixties chief executives saw themselves primarily as responsible for keeping the house in good order and avoiding risk. All too often, large support systems composed of layers of managers and supervisors were introduced into organizations. The 1970s began to see a gradual change in the good times. The oil crisis, interest-rate fluctuations and growing technological advancements contributed to a new uncertainty and challenge to business leaders of the day. Most significantly, America feared a sudden major inflow of competition, both from overseas and in its own market. The 1980s transformed that fear into reality: global competition.

In the United States, chief executive officers, with the vitality of their enterprises at stake, have moved to a new set of standards. The challenge now facing CEOs is to maintain their share of the market, not to increase it. In a market where there is too much capacity, quality, not quantity is the key to survival. Market leadership, quality excellence, high profits and excellent stock prices are the new measures, and these measures must be met, even at he expense of good relations with and loyalty to workers, structures, factories and communities. Monolithic factories owned by major enterprises are giving way to smaller units geographically spread out in the United States and beyond, often in some form of shared ownership with a foreign company. And the old business leader who could afford to be community spokesman and statesman is giving way to the new executive who, in order to ensure the company's survival, must be ruthless in his actions. Often drastic measures are required: slashing unnecessary costs; closing down semi-productive plants; throwing out products and services that are unprofitable; removing tiers of management and supervisory personnel to form "flat" organizational structures; paying for performance and productivity improvement.

Hands-on management is back, as is management consensus and the team approach. They have to be; the decisions are too varied and complex for one person to make. Chief executive officers must do everything possible to run a profitable business, and at the same time work with their teams to plan for tomorrow, knowing that parts of their current operation will probably not be viable in the future.

The results of recent surveys clearly suggest that there is
a feeling that America's competitiveness is declining—largely because of the performance of its business managers.
Basic values—the work ethic and pride in quality—have
slipped. It is also clear that it is up to American executives
to respond to the problem. There are signs this is happening.

Canada faces much the same situation: Canadian
businesses must have the ability to compete in world
markets to survive. Canada's economic realities are changing with the world's. The exponential growth of science
and technology is causing a five- to six-year obsolescence
of today's products. Our organized institutions, including
our governments, can't cope or keep up. Changing world
finance and trade flows are beginning to affect us. Capital
flows now outnumber trade flows by ten to fifteen times.
Decentralization of control and deregulation are world
trends which have hit Canada. To survive our corporations
will have to enter the new game of worldwide marketing,
research, finance and production—the new global ventures.

But can Canadian CEOs change and adopt these new
management methods? More specifically, can we compete
with our American cousins? This is an important question
to consider, especially since at the time of writing, the
debate on free trade between the two countries is raging
across Canada.

Canadian CEOs are optimistic, but admit that the challenge is, at the least, formidable. Michel Bélanger of the
National Bank of Canada believes American managers
have more discipline and more vigor because they have
been more exposed to competition. Yet, he said, "I can
think of quite a number of Canadian chief executives who
are just as good, if not better than anybody you can find in
the States."

Donald McIvor formerly of Imperial Oil has worked on
both sides of the border. He said of American executives:

The average American executive doesn't screw around as
much with external considerations. He is more prone to be ex-

tremely involved in his business. Americans are less diverted than Canadians are from the main cause of their business— namely to protect the interests of the shareholder, despite political pressure to focus on the public good. I think it is part of our tradition of being more closely involved with the state than the average American likes to feel that he is.

Yet Steven Wilgar, who has experience on both sides of the border as president of Warner-Lambert, said:

Canadian executives do not have the cadre of staff that one finds in most American companies, and have consequently had to develop broader business skills. Canadian managers focus more on the consumer and the community. Perhaps they see more of the picture than their counterparts in the U.S. The problems we're seeing in American companies today are there principally because they've ignored those elements.

What seems to give the American chief executive officer the edge? Richard Thomson of the Toronto-Dominion Bank thinks one reason is that the Canadian CEO faces a tougher environment. He told us:

In some ways I think life is more difficult for the Canadian executive. He doesn't have the market position that the U.S. executive has going for him. He has a tougher environment to operate in because our cost structure here can be so frustrating. In many parts of the United States they have few checks on them, compared to our checks here from our social system and our labor situation. Governments make it difficult to do business in Canada compared to the United States, and it's getting worse. Just dealing with our currency presents some unusual problems; we face higher interest rates, for example, than the American executive, and the cost of capital is higher. Our transportation problems are more difficult; our weather is more difficult. There are a lot of things that require Canadian executives to be more innovative and entrepreneurial. Yet they may not be seen as being as aggressive as their American counterparts.

If the American executive is more effective, it is the result of a more competitive environment, said Robert Hurlbut.

I would say that basically the Americans are more demanding of themselves and their organizations. They work longer and harder and are more disciplined. There is no question in my mind that the United States still represents a
community where free enterprise is respected and is an essential ingredient of their society. We tend to be more comfortable here; we look to our creature comforts more.

Louis Hollander returned to the theme of leadership and
the strong emphasis on that value south of the border.

There, the CEOs really are leaders. They really lead the
company where they think it should go. I have seen much
less of that here. My assessment is that a number of
Canadian CEOs are custodians rather than leaders. There
are a lot of CEOs in the U.S. who would not spend a quarter
or half their time in all these various organizations that
people in Toronto do. They just don't have time; they are
there to run their business. One of the problems we have in
Canada is that so much of our industry is managed, not
led, by people who are just carrying out what somebody
else has done in the States.

John Fraser of Federal Industries, which has investments in
both countries, sounded a similar warning.

In my view, one of the fundamental problems of Canada is
management. There are exceptions and there are many
damn smart guys in Canada. But if you take a general look
at Canadian business, you will find entrepreneurial
management is frequently lacking. When I hear people
blaming our lack of productivity on unions, I get quite
angry and frustrated. The problem in this country has nothing to do with the worker. The Canadian worker is one of
the finest in the world, but unfortunately I wouldn't say
that about Canadian management. We are particularly
weak in industrial management and I blame this on the
school system where we seem to turn out great lawyers, accountants and good consultants. But try to find yourself a
foreman to run a manufacturing plant. Or a qualified plant
manager. Some CEOs are costing their shareholders millions
and millions of dollars because they haven't got the guts to

make tough decisions and because they are not prepared to work hard themselves.

Canadian CEOs do not, generally speaking, see themselves as being as strong as their American counterparts. David McCamus offered a thoughtful assessment of the reason for this:

> In my view, the biggest problem with Canada is our self-image and lack of self-confidence. Americans exude more self-confidence, whether they should or not. That's part of the culture down there. Whereas Canadians are a little more inclined to step back; they're less willing sometimes to step out and take risks. That's almost bred into the social framework. Look at our social system; it's based on a low-risk, low-median approach to life. It's designed to appeal to those people who have lower economic aspirations, but who want a secure existence. Whereas the U.S. system is designed on the opposite proposition.

James Burns of Power Financial Corporation looks to the younger Canadian CEO:

> Probably the newer CEOs in Canada would be very much closer to the American model. Why not? They probably went to school there and they seem to be driven by about the same kind of ambitions.

Many Canadian corporations haven't sat still in the midst of change or failed to meet the new global challenge. Northern Telecom is a recognized world leader in telecommunications equipment, aggressively pursuing new markets, products and technologies. It is but one example of Canadian-based international entrepreneurship. Significant numbers of Canadian corporations have met the difficult task of introducing productivity-improvement measures and substantially reducing the layers of managers and supervisory personnel in order to bring costs in line with reality. Even the major Canadian financial institutions, for so long impervious to such tactics, have streamlined their operations. For example, Edward Crawford, the quiet and determined head of Canada Life, established an internal project team of top management, who in turn, through careful analysis, found scores of opportunities to improve productivity and save substantial dollars. Raymond Cyr, when he was the forceful CEO of Bell Canada, established new initiatives to encourage hundreds of Bell employees to take early retirement or seek new job opportunities elsewhere, thus disproving the idea that regulated industries are protected from bad times.

Canadian companies have demonstrated a willingness to revamp their operations and challenge old values. New technologies are being eagerly sought to cut costs and improve quality. Large corporate headquarters are being cut back to just a few key support personnel. Negotiations with unions are far tougher, as are the settlements being made. Far less time is being spent on social concerns, and fewer top executives are seen lunching at their private clubs. More and more are too busy, immersed in the details of running their business. Whether these Canadians are doing it as aggressively as their American counterparts is a moot point, but they are changing and they are motivated.

Comparing Canadian and American CEOs, David Clark, Canadian CEO of Campbell Soup, said:

> As I see it there are a couple of things going to stand us in good stead in the future. One is the fact that our scale has forced us to be more flexible in the way that we run our businesses and set up our manufacturing and so forth. We are bred and born on quick change and short runs. In the U.S. particularly, coming out of the fifties, the critical success factor was to get homogeneous products and turn out a ton of them at the lowest possible unit cost. That means long runs and relatively rigid plants. The way manufacturing is going now, as shown by the Japanese, is quick runs, segmented markets, infinitesimal combinations and permutations of options, almost an individually tailored product if you are in big goods. In the case of packaged goods, like ours, it's niche marketing. The mass markets are literally drying up and disappearing. That's happening around the world, not just in Canada. Canada is the world's original niche market.

The second thing that's going to stand us in good stead has to do with our social and political environment. We have a much more humanistic approach. That's both a strength and a weakness. The strength part of it is that, as businesses come to recognize that humanizing pays off, Canadian managers are beautifully suited to take advantage of that.

The third strength is that we turn out a disproportionate number of generalists relative to our size. That is because Canadian managers, from day one, wear seven hats. We are not very deep in terms of narrow technical understanding. We have to go to experts for that, but we sure are broad!

The change is timely because the 1990s will undoubtedly bring a whole new set of dramatic challenges. The wealthiest nations will get wealthier. Fifteen percent of the world's population will earn more than two-thirds of the world's income. New technology, specifically robotics, will design labor out of the work system. Genetic engineering will have major impacts on pharmaceuticals and agricultural production. Trends in photonics, that is, the emergence of information via optical transmitters and fibers, will make today's products, such as copper cable, obsolete. Better product designs will emerge. Knowledge industries, such as the growing service-industry sector, which is a hundred percent knowledge utilization and zero percent raw materials, will increase. Some large enterprises will fold and small business will continue to be the job creator.

All these changes will have a dramatic impact on nations and the corporations within them. To improve their standard of living, countries will have to invest in higher and knowledge-intensive education. Large companies will have to seek world markets and focus on market share, recognizing that profit is residual. Management will have to invest in technology as a leading edge, and and invest in a growing global economy through innovative joint ventures.

The nineties will challenge Canadian CEOs to turn their corporations into global businesses. The notion of compartmentalized national markets will disappear, and the global marketplace will be a reality. Money and ideas can move around the world in seconds. Satellites have added a new dimension to communications. The result is that people all over the world will know and want what is available in other parts of the globe. That leads to trade. Inevitably today's free flow of capital and knowledge will bring more multinational corporations into the global market. In what will be a very competitive market, it will not really matter where these multinationals are headquartered; to survive they will have to operate under the same economic and political rules that apply to their competitors.

Canadian-based corporations will have to exist and grow in this global market because the material well-being of Canadians will depend on it. While these corporations loom large in Canadian eyes, they are very small on the world scene. Canada's number-one giant, General Motors of Canada, is the fortieth largest non-U.S.-based industrial in the world. Only two other Canadian giants are in the top fifty—Canadian Pacific and Ford Motor Company of Canada. Our Canadian financial institutions are dwarfed by foreign competitors—and to a lesser extent the same is true of those in the United States. The smallest of the top nine Japanese banks is three times as big as the American banking giant CitiCorp, on a market capitalization basis. This is not to say that Canadian corporations are not world class in certain sectors. We earlier mentioned Northern Telecom. Add to that Rio Algom Ltd., and Seagrams, and Abitibi-Price Inc., to name a few others.

That all adds up to a very tough challenge for Canadian chief executive officers in the 1990s. We asked many CEOs what they felt were the keys to being a successful business leader in the future. Laurent Beaudoin of Bombardier believes the next decade will call for greater management involvement and very sound judgment. Ross Johnson agreed. He said: "The toughest thing in business is to predict. So new CEOs have to be faster because they can't slow the pace of the marketplace."

Michael Cornelissen of Royal Trustco sees the role of the CEO becoming far more complex. The days of promotion based on age and years of service are gone forever, he thinks. The new role, responsibilities and complexity of the job require people with incisive minds, education and communication skills and energy and a willingness to accept and implement change. He believes that many of these individuals may come from outside the organizations. He also believes that no CEO should lead an organization for more than ten years. Fresh ideas and new directions are essential to retain the vitality of the organization, says Cornelissen, regardless of the skills of any one individual.

Alan Marchment commented on enduring values:

> When I think of CEOs, I think of leadership, and then my mind goes back a couple of thousand years to the Romans and the Greeks. I don't think we've changed. We're dealing with different things and different techniques in operating a business, but I don't think the essential qualities of leadership change.

Rowland Frazee, now retired from the Royal Bank of Canada, has years of experience to draw on. He commented on the new generation of CEOs:

> I think we do have a new breed, a younger generation coming up now who are better educated. One thing that is not going to change is the ability to choose and to manage good people. The ability of a chief executive to assemble good people around him will be of even greater importance in the future. The changes that will happen, I think, are in the internationalization of business, and I'm talking about major corporations in Canada. It distresses me when I hear some people expressing grave concerns about trade talks with the United States, because what they're almost doing is opting for the status quo. The future CEO will have to appreciate the impact of technology. He will also have to spend more time being aware of government, which will continue to intervene in the marketplace.

Irving Ludmer of Steinberg Inc. stresses the need to return to the basic values of quality and customer service:

We are not really needed, and if we want to make a place for ourselves, it is only by serving people. The only way that I have ever found is through good hard work and in satisfying the customer. When you really get down to it, it's how well you can produce for that customer, and in the course of so doing, there are going to be a few people who are going to try to knock you off, because by trying to serve that customer better you are going to disrupt their world. When they try to do that, you had better be up to it. It is as simple as that. That's what the capitalistic system is all about, and more power to it. I enjoy it. I think it's terrific.

We believe that chief executive officers of Canadian corporations over the years have demonstrated some very similar characteristics. In each generation, the leaders have obviously been very much creatures of their environment. Many of the older generation grew up in the Depression, not a few served through all or parts of World War Two, and in fact some really began their careers quite late in life. Hard work, loyalty, self-discipline and respect for authority were ingrained values, and for some ambition and aggressiveness were seen as negative values. Working hard and doing your best were the keys to advancement.

The newer generation is a different breed. They were born in the late thirties and the forties for the most part, and their parents wanted to give them what they had missed. Life was exciting; jobs were available. Communications were modern; travel was easy. Technological change was everywhere. This generation of business leaders no longer needed to depend on the written word and radio voice. Television and Marshall McLuhan's world had arrived. These people grew up in the fifties and sixties, when Canada enjoyed its greatest economic boom. Greater mobility, more opportunities, increased knowledge, high technology were facts of life. Loyalty and other traditions were less evident.

Corporations soaked up the new, well-educated young men and women, promoted them quickly and rewarded their energy, aggressiveness and ambition. The young, in turn, began to want power and prestige and the rewards that go with them. Now another change in climate has returned corporate America to the basics. And the nineties will bring yet more change.

The new era will require innovation, risk-taking and enormous energy as Canadian corporations seek niches in which to be competitive in international markets. Truly multinational corporations produce executives who believe in the need to develop competitive, open international markets because they are worldly people.

While there are some notable exceptions, not too many of today's CEOs fit that description. The younger generation of CEOs in Canada should be better prepared for the challenge of competing in a global market since they have had greater exposure to business during a period of accelerating change and new worldwide competition.

The question is: can the new generation of Canadian CEOs pull it off? Can they make their enterprises truly competitive in the global market of the future? We believe that the answer to this question will rest on several things:

- CEOs must achieve a balance between social values and the corporate imperative of profitability. Canada's social fabric tends to lead to broader thinking and more compassionate CEOs, whether of the older or younger generation. The potential hazard is that this less narrow focus will lead to a competitive disadvantage in world markets. Canadian CEOs' concern for economic altruism may hinder profitability and productivity.

- Boards of directors must be more vigorous in the demands they make on their CEOs, whether they are chairmen of the boards or not. They must establish realistic standards of performance and ensure that those standards are met. To grow in world markets, major Canadian companies will need all the leadership they can get, and that will require a strong, positive linking of the talents of the board, the CEO and the organization.

- CEOs must realize that they can best meet those demands and manage complex business issues only by working with a trusted and competent team of executives. They will have to do a better job of learning the art of effectively drawing upon the talents of their teams.

- Women managers and executives must be recognized and welcomed. They are proving that, compared to their male counterparts, they are more focused and disciplined and perhaps even more logical in problem-solving. They work more effectively with the time they have available, and have proven themselves committed and effective managers.
- Young people who wish to move up the corporate ladder must be prepared to work hard. Regardless of gender, young people will be facing fierce competition and rapid changes in technology, products and services as they move up the corporate ladder. This will bring not only increased opportunity but also more demands on their time and energy, and will require more risk and more discipline.

The next generation of senior executives must become worldly in a true business sense. This will mean an investment in time and money for training and development in international business, finance, economics, public policy and language skills. It will mean providing opportunities for young managers to go overseas and experience other business environments through transfers and exchange programs. It will mean opening up the corporation to new thoughts and approaches to international growth. It will, above all, require a real commitment on the part of today's CEOs to think internationally.

Executives must enhance their sense of Canada's capacity to compete. Despite our self-deprecating attitudes, the world standing of corporate-size Canadian companies in many industries ranks with the best. We need optimism—in our corporations and in our country. Trevor Eyton sums it up best:

> I'm very optimistic about Canada. It may not have the largest military force or the biggest and fastest satellite, but it will, I think, be a wonderful country and it will continue to afford a quality and standard of living that will be envied by most of the world. I think we have many natural advantages here, including people, particularly our young people. I have a lot to do with one university and I can tell

you from what I see there that we have a lot of dedicated, intelligent, hard-working people in both the student and faculty bodies. I think the greatest need we have in Canada is to spend considerably more money and time and attention on our education. We have to educate better; if we do, we should be able to stand up to anybody. We have an exceptional country that offers a great deal to its people.

A P P E N D I X

L I S T
O F   C E O S
I N T E R V I E W E D

Bandeen, Robert,
Born: 1930, Rodney, Ontario
B.A., University of Western Ontario, Ph.D., Duke University
CEO, Canadian National Railways, 1974 to 1982
CEO, Crown Life Insurance Co., 1982 to 1985.

Beaudoin, Laurent
Born: 1938, Laurier Station, Quebec
M. Comm., University of Sherbrooke, C.A.
CEO, Bombardier, Inc., 1966 to present

Bélanger, Michel F.
Born: 1929, Levis, Quebec
B.A., Laval University, B.Soc. Sc. (Economics), Laval University
CEO, National Bank of Canada, 1979 to present

Blundell, William R.C.
Born: 1927, Montreal, Quebec
B.A. Sc., University of Toronto
CEO, CAMCO Limited, 1979-1983
CEO, Canadian General Electric Company Limited, 1985 to
    present

Burns, James W.
Born: 1929, Winnipeg, Manitoba
B. Comm., University of Manitoba, M.B.A., Harvard University
CEO, Great West Life Assurance Co., 1971 to 1979
CEO, Power Financial Corporation 1984 to present

Charron, André
Born: 1923, Montreal, Quebec
B.A., College Ste. Marie, LL.L., University of Montreal
CEO, Levesque, Beaubien, Inc., 1967 to 1986

Clark, David C.
Born: 1939, Hamilton, Ontario
B.A., McMaster University, M.B.A., University of Western Ontario
CEO, Thomas J. Lipton, Inc., 1982 to 1983
CEO, Campbell Soup Company Ltd., 1983 to present and
    Executive V.P., International Campbell Soup Co.

Cornelissen, Michael A.
Born: 1943, Durban, South Africa
C.A., University of Natal, M.B.A., University of Capetown
CEO, Royal Trust, 1983 to present

Crawford, Edward H.
Born: 1925, Truro, Nova Scotia
B.A., University of Toronto
CEO, Canada Life Assurance Co., 1973 to present

Crawford, Purdy
Born: 1931, Five Islands, Nova Scotia
B.A., Mount Allison, LL.B., Dalhousie, LL.M., Harvard
CEO, Imasco Limited, 1986 to present

Cyr, J. V. Raymond
Born: 1934, Montreal, Quebec
B.A. Sc., University of Montreal
CEO, Bell Canada Limited 1984 to 1987

de Grandpré, A. Jean
Born: 1921, Montreal, Quebec
B.A., College Jean de Brebeuf, B.C.L., McGill University
CEO, Bell Canada 1976 to 1983
CEO, Bell Canada Enterprises, 1983 to present

Demone, Robert S.
Born: 1932, Dartmouth, Nova Scotia
B. Comm., Dalhousie University, C.A.
CEO, Maple Leaf Mills Limited, 1984 to 1987
CEO, Canadian Pacific Hotels Limited, 1987 to present

Eyton, John Trevor
Born: 1934, Quebec City, Quebec
B.A., University of Toronto, LL.B., University of Toronto
CEO, Brascan Limited, 1979 to present

Farquhar, Gordon N.
Born: 1923, Sandy Spring, Maryland, U.S.
B.A., Yale University, LL.B., University of Connecticut
CEO, Aetna Canada, 1974 to 1986

Frazee, Rowland Cardwell
Born: 1921, Halifax, Nova Scotia
B. Comm., Dalhousie University
CEO, Royal Bank of Canada, 1979 to 1986

Fraser, John Foster
Born: 1930, Saskatoon, Saskatchewan
B. Comm., University of Saskatchewan
CEO, Norcom Homes Limited, 1969 to 1978
CEO, Federal Industries Limited, 1978 to present

Galt, Thomas M.
Born: 1921, Winnipeg, Manitoba
B. Comm., University of Manitoba, FSA, FCIA
CEO, Sun Life Assurance Co. of Canada, 1973 to present

Ghert, Bernard I.
Born: 1939, Lethbridge, Alberta
B. Sc., McGill University, M.B.A., University of British Columbia
CEO, Cadillac Fairview Corporation, 1984 to 1987

Gordon, John Peter George
Born: 1920, Toronto, Ontario
B. Sc. (Mech. Eng.), University of Toronto
CEO, Stelco Inc., 1973 to 1984

Gratton, Robert
Born: 1943, Montreal, Quebec
LL.L., University of Montreal, LL.M., London School of
    Economics
M.B.A., Harvard University
CEO, Montreal Trust Company, 1982 to present

Hantho, Charles Harold
Born: 1931, Lethbridge, Alberta
B. Sc. (Chem. Eng.), University of Alberta
CEO, C-I-L Inc., 1982 to present

Hawkrigg, Melvin Michael
Born: 1930, Toronto, Ontario
B.A. McMaster University, F.C.A.
CEO, Fuller Brush Company, 1968 to 1971
CEO, Trilon Financial Corporation, 1984 to present

Heisey, William Lawrence
Born: 1930, Toronto, Ontario
B.A., University of Toronto, M.B.A., Harvard University
CEO, Harlequin Enterprises Limited, 1970 to 1982

Hobbs, Gerald Henry Danby
Born: 1921, Vancouver, British Columbia
CEO, Western Canada Steel, 1968 to 1972
Chairman, Cominco Ltd., 1980 to 1982

Hollander, Louis
Born: 1934, Montreal, Quebec
B. Eng. (Chem.), McGill University, M.B.A., University of
    Western Ontario
CEO, Reichold Ltd., 1982 to 1985
CEO, Canada Colors and Chemicals Limited, 1986 to present

Hurlbut, Robert St. Clair
Born: 1924, Toronto, Ontario
B.A., University of Toronto, Barrister and Solicitor, Osgood Hall
    Law School
CEO, General Foods Inc., 1967 to 1984

Jodoin, Maurice
Born: 1939, Montreal, Quebec
B.A., University of Montreal, L.Sc.Comm., L'Ecole des Hautes
    Etudes Commerciales.
CEO, General Trustco Canada, 1983 to present

Johnson, F. Ross,
Born: 1931, Winnipeg, Manitoba
B. Comm., University of Manitoba, M.B.A., University of Toronto
CEO, Standard Brands Canada Ltd., 1971 to 1973
CEO, Standard Brands Inc., 1976 to 1981
CEO, Nabisco Brands Inc., 1984 to 1985
CEO, RJR Nabisco Inc., 1986 to present

Kadlec, Robert Edward
Born: 1933, Calgary, Alberta
B. Sc., University of Toronto
CEO, Inland Natural Gas Company Limited, 1982 to present

Kavanagh, Kevin Patrick
Born: 1932, Brandon, Manitoba
B. Comm., University of Manitoba
CEO, Great West Life Assurance Company, 1979 to present

Latimer, Radcliff R.
Born: 1933, Florence, Ontario
B. Sc., McGill University, M.B.A., University of Western Ontario
CEO, Trans Canada Pipe Lines Limited, 1979 to 1985

Lodge, Lorne
Born: 1930, Toronto, Ontario
B. Comm., University of Toronto, F.C.A.
CEO, I.B.M. Canada Ltd., 1972 to 1987

Ludmer, Irving
Born: 1935, Montreal, Quebec
B. Eng. (Physics), McGill University
CEO, Steinberg Inc., 1985 to present

Marchment, Alan Ross
Born: 1927, Toronto, Ontario
B.A., University of Toronto, F.C.A.
CEO, Guaranty Trust Company of Canada, 1973 to present
CEO, Traders Group Limited, 1979 to present
CEO, Guaranty Trustco Limited, 1984 to present

Martin, Robert W.
Born: 1936, Toronto, Ontario
B.A.Sc., University of Toronto
CEO, Consumers' Gas Company Ltd., 1984 to present

McCamus, David Robert
Born: 1931, Walkerton, Ontario
B.Comm., University of Toronto
CEO, Xerox Canada Inc., 1982 to present

McCarthy, Donald
Born: 1930, Hornepayne, Ontario
M.B.A. Equivalent, Imede, Switzerland
CEO, Beatrice Foods Inc., 1985 to present

McGiverin, Donald
Born: 1924, Calgary, Alberta
B.Comm., University of Manitoba, M.B.A., Ohio State University
CEO, The Hudson's Bay Company, 1974 to 1985

McIvor, Donald
Born: 1928, Winnipeg, Manitoba
B.Sc., University of Manitoba
CEO, Imperial Oil Limited, 1982 to 1985

Morison, Robert David
Born: 1930, Toronto, Ontario
FCA
CEO, Consumers Packaging Company Limited, 1973 to present

Muncaster, Dean
Born: 1933, Sudbury, Ontario
B.A., University of Western Ontario, M.B.A., Northwestern
   University
CEO, Canadian Tire Corporation Ltd., 1966 to 1985

Peters, Angela Cantwell
Born: 1930, St. John's, Newfoundland
CEO, Bowering Brothers Limited, 1979-1983

Richards, William
Born: 1926, Winnipeg, Manitoba
B.A., LL.B., University of Manitoba
President, Dome Petroleum Limited, 1974-1983

Stock, Valentine Norbert
Born: 1923, Toronto, Ontario
B.A.Sc., University of Toronto
CEO, Canadian Corporate Management, 1972 to 1978
CEO, Canada Packers Inc., 1980 to 1987

Taylor, Allan R.
Born: 1932, Prince Albert, Saskatchewan
CEO, The Royal Bank of Canada, 1986 to present

Thomson, Richard Murray
Born: 1933, Winnipeg, Manitoba
B. Applied Sc. (Eng.), University of Toronto, M.B.A., Harvard
    University
CEO, The Toronto Dominion Bank, 1977 to present

Wilgar, Steven Allan
Born: 1938, Toronto, Ontario
B.A., Bishop's University, M.B.A., University of Western Ontario
CEO, Warner-Lambert Canada Inc., 1974 to 1981 and 1986
    to present

Wilson, Lynton Ronald
Born: 1940, Port Colborne, Ontario
B.A., McMaster University, M.A., Cornell University
CEO, Redpath Industries Ltd., 1981 to present

Wood, Donald
Born: 1935, Montreal, Quebec
B.Comm., McGill University
CEO, Crowntek Inc., 1985-1987

BIBLIOGRAPHY

Bacon, Jeremy and James K. Brown. "Corporate Directorship Practices: Role, Selection and Legal Status of the Board." *The Conference Board, Inc.* (1975).

Bennis, Warren and Bart Nanus. *Leaders.* New York: Harper & Row, 1985.

Burke, W. Warner. *Current Issues and Strategies in Organization Development.* New York: Human Sciences Press, 1977.

The Conference Board. "Corporate Culture and Change." *The Conference Board, Inc.*, Report No. 888 (1986).

————. "Executive Briefing Book on the Business Environment, 1985-1990." *The Conference Board, Inc.* (1985).

————. "Executive Compensation: Issues and Directions." *The Conference Board in Canada* (1979).

Drucker, Peter F. *The Frontiers of Management, Where Tomorrow's Decisions Are Being Shaped Today.* Toronto: Fitzhenry & Whiteside, 1986.

Fisch, Gerald G. *Organization for Profit.* New York: McGraw-Hill Book Company, 1964.

Fraser, John F. "The Party's Over." *Business Quarterly* (1985).

Frost, Peter J., Vance F. Mitchell and Walter R. Nord. *Organizational Reality, Reports From the Firing Line.* Santa Monica: Goodyear Publishing Company, 1978.

Geneen, Harold. *Managing.* New York: Avon Books, 1984.

Golding, Charles William. *What It Takes to Get to the Top and Stay There.* New York: Putnam, 1983.

Greenwalt, Crawford H. *The Uncommon Man: The Individual in the Organization.* New York: McGraw-Hill, 1976.

Handly, Charles B. *Understanding Organizations.* Harmondsworth, England: Penguin Books, 1976.

Harmon, Frederick G. and Garry Jacobs. *The Vital Difference, Unleashing the Powers of Sustained Corporate Success.* New York: AMACOM, 1985.

Hickman, Craig R. and Michael A. Silva. *Creating Excellence.* London: Unwin Paperbacks, 1985.

Jennings, Eugene E. *Routes to the Executive Suite.* New York: McGraw-Hill, 1976.

Levinson, Harry and Stuart Rosenthal. CEO: *Corporate Leadership and Action.* New York: Basic Books.

Likert, Rensis. *New Patterns of Management.* New York: McGraw-Hill, 1961.

Lynch, Edith M. *Decades, Lifestyle Changes in Career Expectations.* New York: AMACOM, 1980.

Maccoby, Michael. *The Leader.* New York: Simon & Schuster, 1981.

McCall, Morgan W. Jr. and Michael M. Lombardo. "Off The Track: Why and How Executives Get Derailed." Technical Report 21, Centre for Creative Leadership, North Carolina, 1983.

Mintzberg, Henry. *The Nature of Managerial Work.* New York: Harper & Row, 1973.

Nad, Abraham. *Directorship, Significant Issues Facing Directors: 1985.* U.S.: Directors Publications, Inc., 1985.

Naisbitt, John. *Megatrends.* New York: Warner Books, 1982.

O'Toole, James. *Vanguard Management.* Garden City: Doubleday & Co., 1985.

Pascale, Richard Tanner and Anthony G. Athos. *The Art of Japanese Management.* New York: Simon and Schuster, 1981.

Peters, Thomas J. and Robert H. Waterman Jr. *In Search of Excellence.* New York: Harper & Row, 1982.

Salmon, Paul and Thomas Friedman. *Life and Death on the Corporate Battlefield.* New York: Simon and Schuster, 1982.

Shook, Robert L. *The Chief Executive Officers.* New York: Harper & Row, 1981.

Sloma, Richard S. *How to Measure Managerial Performance.* New York: Macmillan, 1980.

Stieglitz, Harold. "Chief Executives View Their Jobs." *The Conference Board Inc.* (1985).

Toffler, Alvin. *The Third Wave.* New York: William Morrow and Company, 1980.

Touche Ross & Company. *Audit Committees.* 1982.

Towers, David R. and Mary F. Towers. *Making Participation Management Work.* San Francisco: Jossey-Bass, 1983.

INDEX